From the Oval Office

PRAYERS

of the

PRESIDENTS

E PLURIBUS UNUM

From the Oval Office

PRAYERS

of the
PRESIDENTS

Dr. Larry Keefauver

Bridge-Logos
Gainesville, Florida 32614 USA

Published by:
Bridge-Logos
Gainesville, FL 32614
www.bridgelogos.com

Editor: Dr. Larry Keefauver
Production Artist: Cathleen Kwas
Acknowledgements for editing and research: Stephen R. Clark, Amy Bozeman, Lynn Copeland, Bev Browning

Deep gratitude is expressed to the publisher of Bridge-Logos, Guy Morrell, for his vision, support and enthusiasm for this project.

Table of Contents

Appendices

"We have been recipients of the choicest bounties of Heaven. We have been preserved, these many years, in peace and prosperity. We have grown in numbers, wealth, and power as no other nation has ever grown; but we have forgotten God.

"We have forgotten the gracious hand which preserved us in peace, and multiplied and enriched and strengthened us; and we have vainly imagined, in the deceitfulness of our hearts, that all these blessings were produced by some superior wisdom and virtue of our own. Intoxicated with unbroken success, we have become too self-sufficient to feel the necessity of redeeming and preserving grace, too proud to pray to the God that made us.

"It behooves us, then, to humble ourselves before the offended Power, to confess our national sins, and to pray for clemency and forgiveness."

—Abraham Lincoln

That most of the presidents prayed and invoked God's blessings and favor upon these United States and its citizens is a matter of historical record. On the following pages, many of the public and recorded prayers, invocations, proclamations for thanksgiving and prayer, and statements about faith and prayer made by our forty-two presidents have been collected in this one volume so that we might remember and honor the legacy of prayer and the invocations of blessing and faith bestowed upon America by her presidents.

George Washington

Religious background: Anglican

George Washington was born in Westmoreland County, Virginia on February 22, 1732. His youth saw him through training as a surveyor and becoming an adjunct in the militia. After three years in the militia he married Martha Dandridge Custis, and then he settled down as a farmer in Mount Vernon, Virginia.

Washington developed anti-British sentiment in the militia and as a planter due to British commercial restrictions. Opposing the Stamp Act of 1765, he became an organizer of British resistance. This led to his becoming a delegate to the Continental Congress, and his selection as commander-in-chief of the Continental Army in 1775.

Washington was an able general and saw the American Revolutionary War end in 1781. Afterward, he was faced with the decision of using his talents to help dispel the chaos due to the Articles of the Confederation. After presiding over the Constitutional Convention, he gave in to popular demands that he take the first presidency. He was inaugurated into office on April 30, 1789, in New York, which was the first national capital.

During his years in office, Washington sought to unite the nation and establish the authority of the new government at home and abroad. He was reelected to office in 1792 by a unanimous vote, and at the end of his second term, he delivered his Farewell Address on September 17, 1796. Three years later he contracted a severe throat infection and died at Mt. Vernon on December 14, 1799.

Almighty God,

We make our earnest prayer that Thou wilt keep the United States in Thy holy protection: that Thou wilt incline the hearts of the citizens to cultivate a spirit of subordination and obedience to government, and entertain a brotherly affection and love for one another and for their fellow citizens of the United States at large. And finally that Thou wilt most graciously be pleased to dispose us all to do justice, to love mercy, and to demean ourselves with that charity, humility, and pacific temper of mind which were the characteristics of the Divine Author of our blessed religion, and without a humble imitation of whose example in these things we can never hope to be a happy nation. Grant our supplication, we beseech Thee, through Jesus Christ our Lord. Amen.

(A daily prayer of George Washington)

From the Prayer Journal of George Washington:

Almighty God . . .

I yield thee humble and hearty thanks that thou has preserved me from the danger of the night past, and brought me to the light of the day, and the comforts thereof, a day which is consecrated to thine own service and for thine own honor. Let my heart, therefore, Gracious God, be so affected with the glory and majesty of it, that I may not do mine own works, but wait on thee, and discharge those weighty duties thou requirest of me.

Give me grace to hear thee calling on me in thy word, that it may be wisdom, righteousness, reconciliation and peace to the saving of the soul in the day of the Lord Jesus.

Grant that I may hear it with reverence, receive it with meekness, mingle it with faith, and that it may accomplish in me, Gracious God, the good work for which thou has sent it.

Bless my family, kindred, friends and country, be our God and guide this day and forever for His sake, who lay down in the Grave and arose again for us, Jesus Christ our Lord. Amen.

George Washington (1789-1797)

Thanksgiving, 1789:

"It is the duty of all nations to acknowledge the providence of Almighty God, to obey His will, to be grateful for His benefits and humbly implore His protection and favor."

On consecrating liberty:

"It would be peculiarly improper to omit, in this first official act, my fervent supplication to that Almighty Being who rules over the universe, who presides in the councils of nations, and whose providential aids can supply every human defect, that His benediction may consecrate to the liberties and happiness of the people of the United States."

On the Bible:

"Of all the dispositions and habits which lead to political prosperity, religion and morality are indispensable supports. It is impossible to rightly govern the world without God and the Bible."

(September 17, 1796)

On being a Christian:

"To the distinguished character of Patriot, it should be our highest Glory to laud the more distinguished Character of Christian."

(Valley Forge, Pennsylvania, May 2, 1778)

Thanksgiving Proclamation by George Washington, the President of the United States of America on October 3, 1789

Whereas it is the duty of all Nations to acknowledge the Providence of Almighty God, to obey His will, to be grateful for His benefits, and humbly to implore His protection and favor, and Whereas both Houses of Congress have by their joint Committee requested me "to recommend to the People of the United States a day of public thanks-giving and prayer to be observed by acknowledging with grateful hearts the many single favors of Almighty God, especially by affording them an opportunity peaceably to establish a form of government for their safety and happiness."

Now therefore I do recommend and assign Thursday the 26th day of November next to be devoted by the People of these States to the service of that great and glorious Being, who is the beneficent Author of all the good that was, that is, or that will be. That we may then all unite in rendering unto Him our sincere and humble thanks, for His kind care and protection of the People of this country previous to their becoming a Nation, for the signal and manifold mercies, and the favorable interpositions of His Providence, which we experienced in the course and conclusion of the late war, for the great degree of tranquility, union, and plenty, which we have since enjoyed, for the peaceable and rational manner in which we have been enabled to establish constitutions of government for our safety and happiness, and particularly the national One now lately instituted, for the civil and religious liberty with which we are blessed, and the means we have of acquiring and diffusing useful knowledge and in

George Washington (1789-1797)

general for all the great and various favors which He has been pleased to confer upon us.

And also that we may then unite in most humbly offering our prayers and supplications to the great Lord and Ruler of Nations and beseech Him to pardon our national and other transgressions, to enable us all, whether in public or private stations, to perform our several and relative duties properly and punctually, to render our national government a blessing to all the People, by constantly being a government of wise, just and constitutional laws, discreetly and faithfully executed and obeyed, to protect and guide all Sovereigns and Nations (especially such as have shown kindness unto us) and to bless them with good government, peace, and concord. To promote the knowledge and practice of true religion and virtue, and the increase of science among them and us, and generally to grant unto all Mankind such a degree of temporal prosperity as He alone knows to be best.

John Adams

Religious background: Unitarian

John Adams was born in the Massachusetts Bay Colony in October of 1735. He married Abigail Smith Adams, and the couple was known for the amazing correspondence they kept throughout their life together.

Adams was educated at Harvard University and was known as a supporter of the patriot cause. As a lawyer he became a delegate to the First and Second Continental Congresses, and he led in the movement for independence. During the Revolutionary War he served in European diplomatic roles, and helped negotiate the treaty of peace. He served two rather frustrating terms as vice president, and then was elected president in 1797. During this time, the war between the French and British was causing great difficulties for the United States. Adams soon focused his administration on France. Adams avoided war with the French by launching several successful naval campaigns, and negotiations brought an end to the "quasi war."

Sending a peace mission to France brought the full fury of the Hamiltonians against Adams. In the campaign of 1800 the Republicans were united and effective, but the Federalists were badly divided. Yet, Adams polled only a few less electoral votes than Jefferson, who became president.

On November 1, 1800, just before the election, Adams arrived in the new Capital City to take up his residence in the White House. After his term of office, Adams retired to his farm in Quincy and wrote many famous letters to Thomas Jefferson. On July 4, 1826, he whispered his last words: "Thomas Jefferson survives." But Jefferson had died at Monticello a few hours earlier.

And may that Being who is supreme over all, the Patron of Order, the Fountain of Justice and the Protector in all ages of the world of virtuous liberty, continue His blessing upon this nation.

(March 4, 1797)

On November 1, 1800, just before the election, Adams arrived in the new Capital City to take up his residence in the White House. On his second evening in its damp, unfinished rooms, he wrote to his wife:

Before I end my letter, I pray Heaven to bestow the best of Blessings on this House and all that shall hereafter inhabit it. May none but honest and wise Men ever rule under this roof.

John Adams on the Bible:

"It is essential, my son, in order that you may go through life with comfort to yourself, and usefulness to your fellow creatures, that you should form and adopt certain rules and principles, for the government of your own conduct and temper. It is in the Bible, you must learn them, and from the Bible how to practice them. Those duties are to God, to your fellow creatures, and to yourself."

On the blessing of Providence:

"And may that Being who is supreme over all, the Patron of Order, the Fountain of Justice, and the Protector in all ages of the world of virtuous liberty, continue His blessing upon this nation and its Government and give it all possible success and duration consistent with the ends of His providence."

(Inaugural Address, March 4, 1797)

A Proclamation—Fasting, Prayer, and Thanksgiving by John Adams, President of the United States of America on March 7, 1799

This proclamation was given when a serious plague of Yellow Fever crossed the country. In this proclamation, Adams asked the citizens of the United States to set aside Thursday, April 25, 1799, as a day for solemn humiliation, fasting and prayer.

As no truth is more clearly taught in the Volume of Inspiration, nor any more fully demonstrated by the experience of all ages, than that a deep sense and a due acknowledgment of the governing providence of a Supreme Being and of the accountableness of men to Him as the searcher of hearts and righteous distributor of rewards and punishments are conducive equally to the happiness and rectitude of individuals and to the well-being of communities; as it is also most reasonable in itself that men who are made capable of social acts and relations, who owe their improvements to the social state, and who derive their enjoyments from it, should, as a society, make their acknowledgments of dependence and obligation to Him who hath endowed them with these capacities and elevated them in the scale of existence by these distinctions; as it is likewise a plain dictate of duty and a strong sentiment of nature that in circumstances of great urgency and seasons of imminent danger earnest and particular supplications should be made to Him who is able to defend or to destroy; as, moreover, the most precious interests of the people of the United States are still

held in jeopardy by the hostile designs and insidious acts of a foreign nation, as well as by the dissemination among them of those principles, subversive of the foundations of all religious, moral, and social obligations, that have produced incalculable mischief and misery in other countries; and as, in fine, the observance of special seasons for public religious solemnities is happily calculated to avert the evils which we ought to deprecate and to excite to the performance of the duties which we ought to discharge by calling and fixing the attention of the people at large to the momentous truths already recited, by affording opportunity to teach and inculcate them by animating devotion and giving to it the character of a national act.

For these reasons I have thought proper to recommend, and I do hereby recommend accordingly, that Thursday, the 25th day of April next, be observed throughout the United States of America as a day of solemn humiliation, fasting, and prayer; that the citizens on that day abstain as far as may be from their secular occupations, devote the time to the sacred duties of religion in public and in private; that they call to mind our numerous offenses against the Most High God, confess them before Him with the sincerest penitence, implore His pardoning mercy, through the Great Mediator and Redeemer, for our past transgressions, and that through the grace of His Holy Spirit we may be disposed and enabled to yield a more suitable obedience to His righteous requisitions in time to come; that He would interpose to arrest the progress of that impiety and licentiousness in principle and practice so offensive to Himself and so ruinous to mankind; that He would make us deeply sensible that "righteousness exalteth a nation, but sin is a reproach to any people;" that He would turn us from our transgressions and turn His displeasure from us; that He would withhold us from unreasonable discontent, from disunion, faction, sedition, and insurrection; that He would preserve our country from the desolating sword; that He would save our cities and towns from a repetition of those awful pestilential visitations under which they have lately suffered so severely, and that the health of our inhabitants generally may be precious in His sight;

that He would favor us with fruitful seasons and so bless the labors of the husbandman as that there may be food in abundance for man and beast; that He would prosper our commerce, manufactures, and fisheries, and give success to the people in all their lawful industry and enterprise; that He would smile on our colleges, academies, schools, and seminaries of learning, and make them nurseries of sound science, morals, and religion; that He would bless all magistrates, from the highest to the lowest, give them the true spirit of their station, make them a terror to evil doers and a praise to them that do well; that He would preside over the councils of the nation at this critical period, enlighten them to a just discernment of the public interest, and save them from mistake, division, and discord; that He would make succeed our preparations for defense and bless our armaments by land and by sea; that He would put an end to the effusion of human blood and the accumulation of human misery among the contending nations of the earth by disposing them to justice, to equity, to benevolence, and to peace; and that he would extend the blessings of knowledge, of true liberty, and of pure and undefiled religion throughout the world.

And I do also recommend that with these acts of humiliation, penitence, and prayer, fervent thanksgiving to the Author of All Good be united for the countless favors which He is still continuing to the people of the United States, and which render their condition as a nation eminently happy when compared with the lot of others.

Thomas Jefferson

Religious background: No formal affiliation

Jefferson was born in Virginia on April 13, 1743. At William and Mary College and later with the great law teacher, George Wyeth, he studied law and in 1769 he began six years of service as a representative in the Virginia House of Burgesses. In 1772, he married Martha Wayles Skelton and with her had six children with only two surviving childhood—Martha and Mary.

Jefferson became well known in 1774, when he wrote a political pamphlet, A Summary View of the Rights of British America. Arguing on the basis of natural rights theory, Jefferson claimed that colonial allegiance to the king was voluntary. "The God who gave us life," he wrote, "gave us liberty at the same time: the hand of force may destroy, but cannot disjoin them."

Jefferson was elected to the Second Continental Congress, and on June 11, 1776, he was elected to head a committee of five in preparing the Declaration of Independence. He was its primary author and it made him internationally famous. He climbed to pinnacles such as vice president and president of the United States during his prominent career.

In looking back at his public life and career, Jefferson wished to be remembered for his achievements: his service as governor of Virginia, as a

United States minister to France, as secretary of state under George Washington, as vice-president in the administration of John Adams, and as president. He is also remembered for his other accomplishments: the Louisiana Purchase, inventing, his proficiency as an architect, naturalist, and linguist.

Almighty God,

Who has given us this good land for our heritage; We humbly beseech Thee that we may always prove ourselves a people mindful of Thy favor and glad to do Thy will. Bless our land with honorable ministry, sound learning, and pure manners. Save us from violence, discord, and confusion, from pride and arrogance, and from every evil way. Defend our liberties, and fashion into one united people, the multitude brought hither out of many kindreds and tongues. Endow with Thy spirit of wisdom those whom in Thy Name we entrust the authority of government, that there may be justice and peace at home, and that through obedience to Thy law, we may show forth Thy praise among the nations of the earth. In time of prosperity fill our hearts with thankfulness, and in the day of trouble, suffer not our trust in Thee to fail; all of which we ask through Jesus Christ our Lord. Amen.

(March 4, 1805, A National Prayer for Peace)

Thomas Jefferson on God's gift of liberty:

"God who gave us life gave us liberty. And can the liberties of a nation be thought secure when we have removed their only firm basis, a conviction in the minds of the people that these liberties are of the gift of God? That they are not to be violated but with His wrath? Indeed, I tremble for my country when I reflect that God is just; that His justice cannot sleep forever."

On the Bible:

"I have always said and always will say that the studious perusal of the Sacred Volume will make better citizens, better fathers, better husbands… the Bible makes the best people in the world."

On Jesus:

"Of all systems of morality, ancient or modern, which have come under my observation, none appear to be so pure as that of Jesus."

(Thomas Jefferson to William Canby in 1813)

"I hold the precepts of Jesus as delivered by Himself, to be the most pure, benevolent and sublime which have ever been preached to man."

On Christianity:

"The reason that Christianity is the best friend of Government is because Christianity is the only religion that changes the heart."

James Madison

Religious background: Episcopal

M adison was born in 1751, and lived his early life in Orange County, Virginia. He attended Princeton and studied law. In the early years, Madison was a part of the framing of the Virginia Constitution in 1776, served in the Continental Congress, and was a leader in the Virginia Assembly. He served in the state legislature in 1776, and his intelligence brought him the nickname, "Father of the Constitution." In fact, he set up the system of checks and balances in our government and was the chief architect of the Bill of Rights.

He had many political accomplishments in his political career, and in 1801 he was appointed secretary of state by Thomas Jefferson, with whom he developed United States foreign policy.

Madison was elected president in 1808. Madison became embroiled in the trade and shipping embargo problems caused by France and Britain, all of which led to the War of 1812. He was reelected in 1812 and his second term is notable mostly for his impact on the war. Madison helped refresh the United States Army so they could vigorously fight. Other accomplishments included the approval of the charter of the Second Bank of the United States and the first United States protective tariff.

After leaving office, he retired to his Virginia estate, Montpelier, with his wife, Dolley. He spent time writing many articles and letters as well as serving as rector of the University of Virginia. A letter opened after Madison's death in 1836 read: "The advice nearest to my heart and deepest in my convictions is that the Union of the States be cherished and perpetuated."

The War of 1812 prompted these Proclamations for prayer by James Madison:

A Proclamation—Day of Public Humiliation and Prayer by James Madison, President of the United States of America on July 9, 1812

Whereas the Congress of the United States, by a joint resolution of the two Houses have signified a request, that a day may be recommended, to be observed by the people of the United States, with religious solemnity, as a day of public humiliation and prayer;

And whereas such a recommendation will enable the several religious denominations and societies so disposed, to offer, at one and the same time, their common vows and adorations to Almighty God, on the solemn occasion produced by the war, in which He has been pleased to permit the injustice of a foreign Power to involve these United States;

I do therefore recommend a convenient day to be set apart, for the devout purposes of rendering the Sovereign of the Universe, and the

Benefactor of Mankind, the public homage due to His holy attributes; of acknowledging the transgressions which might justly provoke the manifestations of His divine displeasure; of seeking His merciful forgiveness, and His assistance in the great duties of repentance and amendment; and, especially, of offering fervent supplications.

That, in the present season of calamity and war, He would take the American people under His peculiar care and protection; that He would guide their public councils, animate their patriotism, and bestow His blessing on their arms; that He would inspire all nations with a love of justice and of concord, and with a reverence for the unerring precept of our holy religion, to do to others as they would require that others should do to them.

And, finally, that turning the hearts of our enemies from the violence and injustice which sway their councils against us, He would hasten a restoration of the blessings of peace.

(Given at Washington, D.C., the 9th day of July, A. D. 1812)

A Proclamation—Day of Public Humiliation and Prayer by James Madison, President of the United States of America on July 23, 1813

WHEREAS the Congress of the United States, by a joint resolution of the two Houses, have signified a request that a day may be recommended, to be observed by the people of the United States with religious solemnity, as a day of Public Humiliation and Prayer and whereas in times of public calamity, such as that of the war, brought on the United States by the injustice of a foreign government, it is especially becoming, that the hearts of all should be; touched with the same, and the eyes of all be turned to that Almighty Power, in whose hand are the welfare and the destiny of nations: I do, therefore, issue this my Proclamation, recommending to all who shall be piously disposed to unite their teams and voices in addressing, at one and the same time their vows and adorations to the great Parent and Sovereign of the Universe, that they assemble on the second Thursday of September next, in their respective religious congregations, to render him thanks for the many blessings he has bestowed on the people of the United States; that he has blessed them with a land capable of yielding all the necessaries and requisites of human life, with ample means for convenient exchanges with foreign countries; that he has blessed the labors employed in its cultivation and improvement; that he is now blessing the exertions to extend and establish the arts and manufactures; which will secure within ourselves supplies too important to remain dependent on the precarious policy, or the peaceable dispositions of other nations, and particularly that he has blessed the United States with a political constitution founded on the will and authority of the whole people, and guaranteeing to each individual security, not only of his person and his property, but of those sacred rights of conscience, so essential to his present happiness, and so dear to his future hopes:—that with those expressions of devout thankfulness be joined supplications to the same Almighty Power, that he would look down with compassion on our infirmities, that he would pardon our manifold transgressions, and awaken and strengthen in all the wholesome purposes of repentance and amendment; that in this season of trial and calamity, he would preside, in a particular manner over our public councils, and inspire all citizens with a love of their country, and with those fraternal affections and that mutual confidence, which have so happy a tendency to make us safe at home and respected abroad ; and that, as he was graciously pleased, heretofore, to smile on our struggles against the attempts of the government of the empire of which these states then made a part, to wrest from them the rights and privileges to which they were entitled in common with every other part, and to raise them to the station of an independent and sovereign people; so he would now be pleased, in like manner, to bestow his blessing on our arms in resisting the hostile and persevering efforts of the same power to degrade us on the ocean, the common inheritance of all, from rights and immunities, belonging and essential to the American people, as a co-equal member of the great community of independent nations; and that, inspiring our enemies with moderation, with justice and with that spirit of reasonable accommodation, which our country has continued to manifest,

James Madison (1809–1817)

we may be enabled to beat our swords into plough-shares, and to enjoy in peace, every man; the fruits of his honest industry, and the rewards of his lawful enterprise.

If the public homage of a people can ever be worthy the favorable regard of the Holy and Omniscient Being to whom it is addressed, it must be that, in which those who join in it are guided only by their free choice, by the impulse of their hearts and the dictates of their consciences; and such a spectacle must be interesting to all Christian nations; as proving that religion, that gift of Heaven for the good of man, freed from all coercive edicts, from that unhallowed connection with the powers of this world, which corrupts religion into an instrument or an usurper policy of the state, and making no appeal but to reason, to the heart and to the conscience, can spread its benign influence every where, and can attract to the Divine Altar those free will offerings of humble supplication, thanksgiving and praise, which alone can be acceptable to Him whom no hypocrisy can deceive, and no forced sacrifices propitiate.

Upon these principles, and with these views, the people of the United States are invited, in conformity with the resolution aforesaid, to dedicate the day above named to the religious solemnities therein recommended.

(Given at Washington, D.C., this twenty-third day of July

in the year or our Lord one thousand

eight hundred and thirteen.)

A Proclamation—by James Madison, President of the United States on November 16, 1814

The two Houses of the National Legislature having by a joint resolution expressed their desire that in the present time of public calamity and war a day may be recommended to be observed by the people of the United States as a day of public humiliation and fasting and of prayer to Almighty God for the safety and welfare of these States, His blessing on their arms, and a speedy restoration of peace, I have deemed it proper by this proclamation to recommend that Thursday, the 12th of January next, be set apart as a day on which all may have an opportunity of voluntarily offering at the same time in their respective religious assemblies their humble adoration to the Great Sovereign of the Universe, of confessing their sins and transgressions, and of strengthening their vows of repentance and amendment.

They will be invited by the same solemn occasion to call to mind the distinguished favors conferred on the American people in the general health which has been enjoyed, in the abundant fruits of the season, in the progress of the arts instrumental to their comfort, their prosperity, and their security, and in the victories which have so powerfully contributed to the defense and protection of our country, a devout thankfulness for all which ought to be mingled with their supplications to the Beneficent Parent of the Human Race.

That He would be graciously pleased to pardon all their offenses against Him; to support and animate them in the discharge of their respective duties; to continue to them the precious advantages flowing from political institutions so auspicious to their safety against dangers from abroad, to their tranquility at home, and to their liberties, civil and religious; and that He would in a special manner preside over the nation in its public councils and constituted authorities, giving wisdom to its measures and success to its arms in maintaining its rights and in overcoming all hostile designs and attempts against it.

And, finally, that by inspiring the enemy with dispositions favorable to a just and reasonable peace its blessings may be speedily and happily restored.

James Monroe

Religious background: Episcopal

James Monroe was born and raised in Virginia. In early adulthood, he studied law under Thomas Jefferson, and also fought in the American Revolution. He served in the Congress and United States Senate, where he spoke out against George Washington's administration. On becoming U.S. minister to France, he was quickly recalled to the States.

Monroe was thought to be honest to a fault, which further enhanced his career. He became governor of Virginia in 1811 but soon resigned to become secretary of state. He was handsome, energetic and intelligent and was backed by President Madison, all of which made it easy for him to become the Republican choice for the Presidency in 1816. He had little opposition in 1820 and was able to win reelection.

During his stay in office, Monroe presided over a period known as the "Era of Good Feelings." During his administration, Monroe oversaw the Seminole War, and the acquisition of the Floridas in 1819. He also signed the Missouri Compromise in 1820. With the help of John Quincy Adams, he developed the principles of United States foreign policy later called the Monroe Doctrine. He died in 1831.

The liberty, prosperity, and happiness of our country will always to be the object of my most fervent prayers to the Supreme Author of All Good.

(2nd Inaugural Address, March 5, 1821)

James Monroe on the Bible:

"Voltaire spoke of the Bible as a short-lived book. He said that within a hundred years it would pass from common use. Not many people read Voltaire today, but his house has been packed with Bibles as a depot of a Bible society. The Bible rose to the place it now occupies because it deserved to rise to that place, and not because God sent anybody with a box of tricks to prove its divine authority."

On God's blessings:

"For these blessings we owe to Almighty God from whom we derive them, and with profound reverence, our most grateful and unceasing acknowledgments…. That these blessings may be preserved and perpetuated will be the object of my fervent and unceasing prayers to the Supreme Ruler of the Universe.

"For advantages so numerous and highly important it is our duty to unite in grateful acknowledgements to that Omnipotent Being from whom they are derived, and in unceasing prayer that He will endow us with virtue and strength to maintain and hand them down in their utmost purity to our latest posterity."

(1st annual message presented in written form to Congress, December 12, 1817)

John Quincy Adams

Religious background: Unitarian

John Quincy Adams was the 6th president of the United States and the first president who was the son of a president, John Adams He was born in Braintree, Massachusetts, in 1767. In adulthood he became secretary to his father in Europe. This led to his proficiency as a linguist and writer. He graduated Harvard and became a lawyer. Then at age of twenty-six, he was appointed Minister to the Netherlands. In 1802 he was elected to the United States Senate. Later he was appointed Minister to Russia.

Adams served under President James Monroe as Secretary of State. He was elected president in 1824, and he faced much hostility in congress. In 1828, Adams furthered his desire to build connections of highways and canals by breaking ground for the 185-mile C & O Canal.

Adams also desired to use governmental, educational initiatives and funding to establish the United States as a world leader in the arts and science, which was opposed strongly and labeled as transcending "constitutional limitations."

In 1928, Adam's campaign for reelection collapsed under criticism and accusations of corruption and financial misappropriation. This was extremely upsetting to him. He was defeated in the election, and he returned to Massachusetts intent on retiring. His retirement was short-lived as he was elected to the House of Representatives in 1830. He served in this powerful seat for the rest of his life. In 1848 he collapsed while working the Floor of the House and was carried to the Speaker's Room. He died two days later.

As John Quincy Adams aged and grew feeble, he prayerfully consoled himself with these words from Psalm 71:18:

Now also when I am old and grayheaded,
O God, forsake me not;
Until I have shewed my
*   strength,*
Unto this generation,
And power in everyone
*   that is to come.*

Then he made this pious confession:

For I believe there is a
God who heareth prayer and
that honest prayers to him will
not be in vain.

John Quincy Adams on the blessings of Providence:

"In taking a general survey of the concerns of our beloved country, with reference to subjects interesting to the common welfare, the first sentiment which impresses itself upon the mind is of gratitude to the Omnipotent Disposer of All Good for the incontinencies unusual extent that has prevailed within our borders, and for that abundance which the vicissitudes of the seasons has been scattered with profusion over our land. Nor ought we less to ascribe to Him the glory that we are permitted to enjoy the bounties of His hand in peace and tranquility-in peace with all the other nations of the earth, in tranquility among ourselves. There has, indeed, rarely been a period in the history of civilized men in which the general condition of the Christian nations has been marked so extensively by peace and prosperity.

"May I never cease to be grateful for the numberless blessings received through life at His hands, never repine at what He has denied, never murmur at the dispensations of Providence, and implore His forgiveness for all the errors and delinquencies of my life!"

(Starting his 1st annual message to
Congress on December 6, 1825)

On Christianity:

"It is not slight testimonial, both to the merit and worth of Christianity, that in all ages since its promulgation the great mass of those who have risen to eminence by their profound wisdom and integrity have recognized and reverenced Jesus of Nazareth as the Son of the living God."

On the Bible:

"My custom is to read four or five chapters of the Bible every morning immediately after rising.... It seems to me the most suitable manner of beginning the day.... It is an invaluable and inexhaustible mine of knowledge and virtue."

Andrew Jackson

Religious background: Presbyterian

Andrew Jackson was born in a small settlement in the Carolinas in 1767. He was not educated in a traditional sense, but in early adulthood he was able to study law and became a brilliant lawyer in Tennessee. He was involved in fighting and duels as a young man, and even killed a man while defending the honor of his wife.

Jackson was a slave owner and did well for himself as his career flourished. He became the first man elected from Tennessee to the House of Representatives, and then he went on to sit in the Senate. In 1812, he became a war hero after a decisive victory at the Battle of New Orleans; he was instantly dubbed "Old Hickory" by the press. The nickname came from a soldier who served with Jackson and remarked that Jackson was "tough as hickory."

Andrews began a fierce fight for the presidency against Adams in 1832. His controversial political views made him popular. He won fifty-six percent of the popular vote in the 1832 election.

Controversy followed Jackson in office. He replaced officeholders with his supporters, a practice of patronage, known as the "spoils system." He also moved Native American tribes westward to Oklahoma with the Indian Removal Acts. Later Jackson had a falling out with his vice president, J. C. Calhoun, who led a movement to give states the right to nullify an act of the national government that was judged to be unconstitutional.

He was reelected in 1832 and became increasingly popular throughout his presidency. The Democratic Party developed which led to the two party system during his administration.

"Old Hickory" retired from his office in 1837, and died in June of 1845 at his Tennessee home, the Hermitage.

'Tis my fervent prayer to that Almighty Being that He will so overrule all my intentions and actions and inspire the hearts of my fellow citizens that we may be preserved from dangers of all kinds and continue forever a united, happy people.

(March 4, 1833)

Andrew Jackson on Scripture:

"We who are frequently visited by this chastening rod, have the consolation to read in the Scriptures that whomsoever He chasteneth He loveth, and does it for their good to make them mindful of their mortality and that this earth is not our abiding; and afflicts us that we may prepare for a better world, a happy mortality."

On the Bible:

"The Bible is the Rock on which this Republic rests."

On the Cross:

"Let us look forward to the time when we can take the flag of our country and nail it below the Cross, and there let it wave as it waved in the olden times, and let us gather around it and inscribe for our motto: 'Liberty and Union, one and inseparable, now and forever', and exclaim: Christ first, our country next!"

On refusing to proclaim a day of humiliation and fasting:

"I could not do otherwise without transcending the limits prescribed by the Constitution for the President and without feeling that I might in some degree disturb the security which religion nowadays enjoys in this country in its complete separation from the political concerns of the General Government."

— letter to the Synod of the Reformed
Church of North America, June 12, 1832

On hell:

Young Nashville lawyer: "Mr. Cartwright, do you believe there is any such place as hell, as a place of torment?"

Rev. Peter Cartwright: "Yes, I do."

Young Nashville lawyer: "Well, I thank God I have too much good sense to believe any such thing."

Andrew Jackson: "Well, sir, I thank God that there is such a place of torment as hell."

Young Nashville lawyer: "Why, General Jackson, what do you want with such a place of torment as hell?"

Andrew Jackson: "To put such damned rascals as you are in, that oppose and vilify the Christian religion."

—date unspecified, from
Autobiography of Peter Cartwright

On God's protection:

"I trust that the God of Isaac and of Jacob will protect you, and give you health in my absence, in him alone we ought to trust, he alone can preserve, and guide us through this troublesome world, and I am sure he will hear your prayers. We are told that the prayers of the righteous prevaileth much, and I add mine for your health and preservation until we meet again."

—letter to his wife, Rachel Jackson, December 21, 1823
(this is typical of Jackson's letters to his wife)

Martin Van Buren

Religious background: Dutch Reformed

Martin Van Buren was of a humble background: he was of Dutch descent and was the son of a tavern keeper. Born in Kinderhook, N.Y., he was raised on a farm. After his education, he practiced law, served in the state senate, and in 1816 became state attorney general.

While in the Senate, Van Buren was instrumental in helping Andrew Jackson get elected president. With Jackson's support and the death of a former rival for office, Van Buren made a successful bid for governor of New York. However, he only held office a short time, leaving the governor's mansion to accept Jackson's offer to serve in his close-knit "Kitchen Cabinet" as Secretary of State.

Nicknamed the "Little Magician" for his political cunning in ousting Vice President John Calhoun from Jackson's ticket during his bid for reelection, Van Buren was elected as Vice President in 1832 and then President in 1836.

Economic depression weighed on his term as president, as did the Maine-Canada border dispute, the Seminole War in Florida, and the debate over the annexation of Texas.

Van Buren had many political views and was strongly antislavery, which affected his bid for reelection. He failed to win the Democratic nomination in 1844. In 1848 he was nominated for president by the Free Soil Party, but was not reelected, again. He died in 1862 in New York.

I only look to the gracious protection of that Divine Being whose strengthening support I humbly solicit, and whom I fervently pray to look down upon us all.

May it be among the dispensations of His Providence to bless our beloved country with honors and length of days; may her ways be pleasantness, and all her paths peace!

(Inaugural Address, March 4, 1837)

William Henry Harrison

Religious background: Episcopal

W illiam Harrison was born to an affluent political family at Berkley Plantation, Virginia, in 1773. As a young man, he studied medicine at Richmond, then changed directions at the age of 18 and enlisted in the army. He was part of the fight and victory at the Battle of Fallen Timbers.

In 1798, he became secretary of the Northwest Territories, and then in 1800, he became governor of the new Indiana Territory.

Under pressure from settlers, as their governor, his primary duty as such was to negotiate with Indians for land. When the Indians retaliated, Harrison was responsible for defense, and led the victory at the Battle of Tippecanoe in 1811. This established his reputation with the public, and when he returned to public life, Harrison served in the United States House of Representatives and then in the Senate.

He became a favorite of the Whigs for nomination to the Presidency in 1836, which he lost narrowly. He ran again in 1840 with John Tyler, and their slogan was "Tippecanoe and Tyler, too." They won the election by sweeping the Electoral College.

William Henry Harrison (1841–1841)

At age 68, Harrison delivered one of the longest inaugural speeches in history, and did so in cold weather without a coat or hat. He came down with pneumonia and was in office less than one month when he died on April 4, 1841. He was the first president to die in office.

I deem the present occasion sufficiently important and solemn to justify me in expressing to my fellow citizens a profound reverence for the Christian religion, and a thorough conviction that sound morals, religious liberty, and a just sense of religious responsibility are essentially connected with all true and lasting happiness; And to that good Being who has blessed us by the gifts of civil and religious freedom, who watched over and prospered the labors of our fathers and has hitherto preserved to us institutions far exceeding in excellence those of any other people, let us unite in fervently commending every interest of our beloved country in all future time.

(Inaugural Address, March 4, 1841)

John Tyler

Religious background: Episcopal

William Henry Harrison died one month after taking office, and John Tyler became the first to attain the presidency due to the death of a sitting president. He was dubbed, "His Accidency" on more than one occasion.

John Tyler was born in Virginia in 1790, and there he attended the college of William and Mary where he studied law. He became the 10th president of the United States after serving in the state legislature, as governor of Virginia, in the United States House of Representative, and in the Senate.

Even though he was a slaveholder, he tried to prohibit slave trading. He broke with the Democratic Party and then was nominated as vice president by the Whig party. He ran under William H. Harrison, and they won the election of 1840. Their campaign slogan was "Tippecanoe and Tyler, too.

In office he vetoed a national bank bill supported by the Whigs, which left him without any support from his party. He also reorganized the Navy, as well as settle the Seminole war in Florida, and he also oversaw the annexation of Texas.

Tyler was nominated for reelection, but withdrew and took to retirement instead. He went on to organize the Washington Peace Conference in 1861. In 1861, when the Civil War began, he came out of retirement to take a seat in the Confederate House of Representatives, but died before he could take office in 1862.

When a Christian people feel themselves to be overtaken by a great public calamity, it becomes them to humble themselves under the dispensation of Divine Providence, to recognize His righteous government over the children of men, to acknowledge His goodness in time past, as well as their own unworthiness, and to supplicate His merciful protection for the future.

(Proclamation following the death of William Henry Harrison, April 13, 1841)

John Tyler on remembering God's protection:

"…We are all called upon by the highest obligations of duty to renew our thanks and our devotion to our Heavenly Parent, who has continued to vouchsafe to us the eminent blessings which surround us and who has so signally crowned the year with His goodness. If we find ourselves increasing beyond example in numbers, in strength, in wealth, in knowledge, in everything which promotes human and social happiness, let us ever remember our dependence for all these on the protection and merciful dispensations of Divine Providence."

(1st Message, Dec. 7, 1841)

On expressing profound gratitude to God:

"We have continued reason to express our profound gratitude to the Great Creator of All Things for numberless benefits conferred upon us as a people. Blessed with genial seasons, the husbandman has his garners filled with abundance, and the necessaries of life, not to speak of its luxuries, abound in every direction. While in some other nations steady and industrious labor can hardly find the means of subsistence, the greatest evil which we have to encounter is a surplus of production beyond the home demand, which seeks, and with difficulty finds, a partial market in other regions. The health of the country, with partial exceptions, has for the past year been well preserved, and under their free and wise institutions the United States are rapidly advancing toward the consummation of the high destiny which an overruling Providence seems to have marked out for them. Exempt from domestic convulsion and at peace with all the world, we are left free to consult as to the best means of securing and advancing the happiness of the people. Such are the circumstances under which you now assemble in your respective chambers and which should lead us to unite in praise and thanksgiving to that great Being who made us and who preserves us as a nation."

(2nd Annual Message to Congress, Dec. 6, 1842)

John Tyler (1841–1845)

On giving thanks to God:

"If any people ever had cause to render up thanks to the Supreme Being for parental care and protection extended to them in all the trials and difficulties to which they have been from time to time exposed, we certainly are that people. From the first settlement of our forefathers on this continent, through the dangers attendant upon the occupation of a savage wilderness, through a long period of colonial dependence, through the War of the Revolution, in the wisdom which led to the adoption of the existing forms of republican government, in the hazards incident to a war subsequently waged with one of the most powerful nations of the earth, in the increase of our population, in the spread of the arts and sciences, and in the strength and durability conferred on political institutions emanating from the people and sustained by their will, the superintendence of an overruling Providence has been plainly visible. As preparatory, therefore, to entering once more upon the high duties of legislation, it becomes us humbly to acknowledge our dependence upon Him as our guide and protector and to implore a continuance of His parental watchfulness over our beloved country."

(3rd Annual Message to Congress, December, 1843)

On expressing gratitude to the Ruler of the Universe:

"We have continued cause for expressing our gratitude to the Supreme Ruler of the Universe for the benefits and blessings which our country, under His kind providence, has enjoyed during the past year."

(4th Annual Message to Congress, Dec. 3, 1844)

James K. Polk

Religious background: Presbyterian

J ames Polk was a studious and industrious young man who would later become the 11th president of the United States. Born in Mecklenburg County, N.C., in 1795, he became a lawyer in Tennessee, and later a supporter of Andrew Jackson. Jackson helped Polk win the election to the United States House of Representatives, and when Polk left the house he became governor of Tennessee.

In 1844, at a deadlocked Democratic convention, Polk was nominated as the compromise candidate. He has since become known as the first "dark horse" presidential candidate.

Polk was elected to the presidency at the age of 49, and was the youngest president up to that time. During his administration he was successful at concluding the Oregon border dispute with Britain in 1846, and he secured passage of the Walker Tariff Act in 1846. When Texas joined the Union in 1845, a boundary dispute with Mexico led to war in 1846. By 1848, when American forces penetrated south to Mexico City, Mexico signed a treaty that gave the United States some 500,000 square miles including land that would become California, Utah, Nevada, New

James K. Polk (1845–1849)

Mexico and Arizona. Unfortunately, this acquisition intensified the dispute over slavery in the territories, a dispute that Polk was not able to resolve.

Polk's administration also created the Department of the Interior, the United States Naval Academy, and the Smithsonian Institution. There was also a point at which the treasury system was revised. Polk was an efficient and talented president. His hard work pushed him into exhaustion and therefore he did not run for reelection. He died three months after leaving office in 1849.

Confidently relying upon the aid and assistance of the coordinate departments of the Government in conducting our public affairs, I enter upon the discharge of the high duties which have been assigned me by the people, again humbly supplicating that Divine Being who has watched over and protected our beloved country from its infancy to the present hour to continue His gracious benedictions upon us, that we may continue to be a prosperous and happy people.

(March 4, 1845 Inaugural Address)

James Polk on God's blessings:

"I am happy that I can congratulate you on the continued prosperity of our country. Under the blessings of Divine Providence and the benign influence of our free institutions, it stands before the world a spectacle of national happiness."

(1st Annual Message to Congress, Dec. 2, 1845)

On acknowledging God's blessings:

"Our devout and sincere acknowledgments are due to the gracious Giver of All Good for the numberless blessings which our beloved country enjoys."

(2nd Annual Message to Congress, Dec. 8, 1846)

On Divine protection:

"No country has been so much favored, or should acknowledge with deeper reverence the manifestations of the divine protection. An all wise Creator directed and guarded us in our infant struggle for freedom and has constantly watched over our surprising progress until we have become one of the great nations of the earth."

(3rd Annual Message to Congress,
Dec. 7, 1847)

On the benign providence of Almighty God:

"Under the benignant providence of Almighty God the representatives of the States and of the people are again brought together to deliberate for the public good. The gratitude of the nation to the Sovereign Arbiter of All Human Events should be commensurate with the boundless blessings which we enjoy."

(4th Annual Message to Congress, Dec. 5, 1848)

Zachary Taylor

Religious background: Episcopal

Zachary Taylor was born in Virginia in 1784, and he was raised on a plantation in Kentucky. He was a career officer in the Army and fought for a quarter of a century. He fought in the War of 1812, the Black Hawk War, and the Seminole War in Florida. Taylor was dubbed "Old Rough-and-Ready" for his strength and indifferent attitude.

In 1948, Taylor became a war hero, and was nominated by the Whig Party for presidential candidate. However, during his term, Taylor refused to be a puppet of any party, including the Whigs. He acted outside of policies and parties and ran his administration much like he would have run a war. He faced territorial controversies that resulted in the Compromise of 1850.

He had an extremely short term due to his untimely death on July 9, 1850 probably of cholera, after only sixteen months in office. He was the second president to die in office.

In conclusion I congratulate you, my fellow-citizens, upon the high state of prosperity to which the goodness of Divine Providence has conducted our common country. Let us invoke a continuance of the same protecting care which has led us from small beginnings to the eminence we this day occupy.

(Inaugural Address, March 5, 1849)

We are at peace with all the other nations of the world, and seek to maintain our cherished relations of amity with them. During the past year we have been blessed by a kind Providence with an abundance of the fruits of the earth, and although the destroying angel for a time visited extensive portions of our territory with the ravages of a dreadful pestilence, yet the Almighty has at length deigned to stay his hand and to restore the inestimable blessing of general health to a people who have acknowledged His power, deprecated His wrath, and implored His merciful protection.

(Annual Message to Congress, Dec. 4, 1849)

12th President of the United States

Millard Fillmore

Religious background: Unitarian

Millard Fillmore was born in a log cabin in 1800 in Locke, New York, where he lived his youth out in the frontier. He was from a very poor family, and he worked on his father's farm. Fillmore had his first job at the age of fifteen as an indentured apprentice to a cloth maker. He was schooled by a redheaded teacher named Abigail Powers, whom he married later in life.

In 1823 he was admitted to the bar after studying law with a local judge. He moved his law office to Buffalo, New York, and began to associate with members of the Whig party. Fillmore held state office and for eight years was a member of the House. He served in the United States House of Representatives, and in 1848 the Whigs nominated Fillmore as vice president. He was elected with Zachary Taylor.

Fillmore became the 13th President on Taylor's death in 1850. During his administration, he supported the Compromise of 1850. He insisted on federal enforcement of the Fugitive Slave Act, even though he hated slavery. This stance alienated the North, and later led to his defeat in the convention of 1852, which consequently ended the Whig party.

Fillmore refused to join the Republican Party, but he did accept a nomination from the "Know Nothing" (or American Party). During the civil war he opposed President Abraham Lincoln, and later supported President Andrew Johnson during reconstruction. After leaving office he died in 1874.

I rely upon Him who holds in His hands the destinies of nations to endow me with the requisite strength for the task and to avert from our country the evils apprehended from the heavy calamity which has befallen us.

God knows I detest slavery.

I have no hostility to foreigners... Having witnessed their deplorable condition in the old country, God forbid I should add to their sufferings by refusing them an asylum in this.

Millard Fillmore on invoking thanks to God:

"And now, fellow-citizens, I can not bring this communication to a close without invoking you to join me in humble and devout thanks to the Great Ruler of Nations for the multiplied blessings which He has graciously bestowed upon us. His hand, so often visible in our preservation, has stayed the pestilence, saved us from foreign wars and domestic disturbances, and scattered plenty throughout the land. Our liberties, religions and civil, have been maintained, the fountains of knowledge have all been kept open, and means of happiness widely spread and generally enjoyed greater than have fallen to the lot of any other nation. And while deeply penetrated with gratitude for the past, let us hope that His all-wise providence will so guide our counsels as that they shall result in giving satisfaction to our constituents, securing the peace of the country, and adding new strength to the united Government under which we live."

(1st Annual Message to Congress, Dec. 2, 1850)

"Our grateful thanks are due to an all-merciful Providence, not only for staying the pestilence which in different forms has desolated some of our cities, but for crowning the labors of the husbandman with an abundant harvest and the nation generally with the blessings of peace and prosperity."

(3rd Annual Message to Congress, Dec. 6, 1852)

Franklin Pierce

Religious background: Episcopal

Franklin Pierce was born on November 23, 1804 in Hillsboro, New Hampshire. After his education he began his career by practicing law, then leaving for Washington and serving in the United States House of Representatives from 1833–1837. He then went on to the Senate. In 1842, Pierce returned to his law practice after briefly serving in the Mexican War.

When Democrats couldn't agree on a presidential candidate, New Hampshire supporters proposed Pierce for the Presidential nomination in 1852. At the Democratic Convention, Pierce was nominated as a true "dark horse" after 48 ballots. During a time of tranquility in the nation, Pierce took office after winning the election unexpectedly. Two months before he took office, his eleven year old son was tragically killed. This left Pierce exhausted and grieving upon becoming President.

In order to keep harmony with the Union, he opposed antislavery agitation to satisfy the Southern opinion. Pierce made way for territorial expansion that resulted in the controversy over the Ostend Manifesto, a proposal to purchase Cuba from Spain. When it appeared that doing so would expand slavery, a furor developed which ended negotiations.

While in office, Pierce fine-tuned the diplomatic and consular service, and he also put into effect the United States Court of Claims. By the time his term was over, Pierce was able to say that things had remained peaceful, but the Democrats weren't as pleased and refused his nomination for a second term. Pierce left for New Hampshire, where he lived out his life until his death in 1869.

But let not the foundation of our hope rest upon man's wisdom. It will not be sufficient that sectional prejudices find no place in the public deliberations. It will not be sufficient that the rash counsels of human passion are rejected. It must be felt that there is no national security but in the nation's humble, acknowledged dependence upon God and His overruling providence...

I can express no better hope for my country than that the kind Providence which smiled upon our fathers may enable their children to preserve the blessings they have inherited.

(Inaugural Address, March 4, 1853)

Franklin Pierce on America being an example of Christendom:

"In the present, therefore, as in the past, we find ample grounds for reverent thankfulness to the God of grace and providence for His protecting care and merciful dealings with us as a people...."

"We have to maintain inviolate the great doctrine of the inherent right of popular self-government; to reconcile the largest liberty of the individual citizen with complete security of the public order; to render cheerful obedience to the laws of the land, to unite in enforcing their execution, and to frown indignantly on all combinations to resist them; to harmonize a sincere and ardent devotion to the institutions of religious faith with the most universal religious toleration....whilst exalting the condition of the Republic, to assure to it the legitimate influence and the benign authority of a great example amongst all the powers of Christendom. Under the solemnity of these convictions the blessings of Almighty God is earnestly invoked to attend upon your deliberations and upon all the counsels and acts of the Government, to the end that, with common zeal and common efforts, we may, in humble submission to the divine will, cooperate for the promotion of the supreme good of these United States."

(2nd Annual Message to Congress, Dec. 4, 1854)

On gratitude to the good Providence:

"I shall prepare to surrender the Executive trust to my successor and retire to private life with sentiments of profound gratitude to the good Providence which during the period of my Administration has vouchsafed to carry the country through many difficulties, domestic and foreign, and which enables me to contemplate the spectacle of amicable and respectful relations between ours and all other governments and the establishment of constitutional order and tranquility throughout the Union."

(4th Annual Message to Congress, Dec. 2, 1856)

James Buchanan

Religious background: Presbyterian

Tall, formal, and reserved, James Buchanan was the only president who remained unmarried. Born near Mercersburg, Pennsylvania, into a prominent family, he was a graduate of Dickinson College. Buchanan was a gifted debater and well-learned in law.

In his early career, he became a lawyer and member of the Pennsylvania legislature before serving in the United States House of Representatives. Then he served as minister to Russia, and then in the United States Senate.

He became secretary of state in President James K. Polk's cabinet. As minister to Britain, in the 1850's, he helped draft the Ostend Manifesto. Servicing abroad helped to bring him the Democratic presidential nomination in 1856 because it had exempted him from involvement in bitter domestic controversies.

In 1856 he secured the Democratic nomination and election as United States president, defeating J. C. Frémont. Though experienced in government and law, he was unable to grasp the political realities of his time, and dealt ineffectively with the slavery crisis. Buchanan adopted a policy of inactivity involving the political issues of his time, and that policy continued until he left office. The effect was a split within his party that allowed Abraham Lincoln to win the election of 1860.

Buchanan denounced the secession of South Carolina following the election and sent reinforcements to Ft. Sumter, but failed to respond further to the mounting crisis. By the end of his term, six other Southern states had seceded with South Carolina from the Union. In March 1861 he retired to his Pennsylvania home in Wheatland. He died seven years later, leaving Lincoln to resolve the standing issues dividing the nation.

In entering upon this great office I must humbly invoke the God of our fathers for wisdom and firmness to execute its high and responsible duties in such a manner as to restore harmony and ancient friendship among the people of the several States and to preserve our free institutions throughout many generations...

"We ought to cultivate peace, commerce, and friendship with all nations, and this not merely as the best means of promoting our own material interests, but in a spirit of Christian benevolence toward our fellow-men, wherever their lot may be cast. In all our acquisitions the people, under the protection of the American flag, have enjoyed civil and religious liberty. I shall now proceed to take the oath prescribed by the Constitution, whilst humbly invoking the blessing of Divine Providence on this great people.

(Inaugural Address, March 4, 1857)

James Buchanan on prayers to the Almighty:

"But first and above all, our thanks are due to Almighty God for the numerous benefits which He has bestowed upon this people, and our united prayers ought to ascend to Him that He would continue to bless our great Republic in time to come as He has blessed it in time past."

(1st Annual Message to Congress, December 8, 1857)

On God's relief in crisis:

"When we compare the condition of the country at the present day with what it was one year ago at the meeting of Congress, we have much reason for gratitude to that Almighty Providence which has never failed to interpose for our relief at the most critical periods of our history."

(2nd Annual Message to Congress, December 6, 1858)

On invoking divine guidance and protection:

"Our deep and heartfelt gratitude is due to that Almighty Power which has bestowed upon us such varied and numerous blessings throughout the past year. The general health of the country has been excellent, our harvests have been unusually plentiful, and prosperity smiles throughout the land. Indeed, notwithstanding our demerits, we have much reason to believe from the past events in our history that we have enjoyed the special protection of Divine Providence ever since our origin as a nation. We have been exposed to many threatening and alarming difficulties in our progress, but on each successive occasion the impending cloud has been dissipated at the moment it appeared ready to burst upon our head, and the danger to our institutions has passed away. May we ever be under the divine guidance and protection."

On the eve of Civil War:

"Self-preservation is the first law of nature, and has been implanted in the heart of man by his Creator for the wisest purpose; and no political union, however fraught with blessings and benefits in all other respects, can long continue if the necessary consequence be to render the homes and the firesides of nearly half the parties to it habitually and hopelessly insecure. Sooner or later the bonds of such a union must be severed. It is my conviction that this fatal period has not yet arrived, and my prayer to God is that He would preserve the Constitution and the Union throughout all generations."

(4th Annual Message to Congress, Decmber 3, 1860)

Abraham Lincoln

Religious background: No formal affiliation

Born in a log cabin, Abraham Lincoln once described his life, saying, "I was born Feb. 12, 1809, in Hardin County, Kentucky. My parents were both born in Virginia, of undistinguished families. It was a wild region, with many bears and other wild animals still in the woods. There I grew up. Of course when I came of age I did not know much. Still somehow, I could read, write, and cipher but that was all."

Though largely self-taught, he practiced law in Springfield, Illinois, and served in the state legislature. He was soon elected as a Whig to the United States House of Representatives, and as a circuit-riding lawyer, he became extremely successful being nicknamed "Honest Abe."

In 1856 he joined the Republican Party, which nominated him to run in 1858 for the state senate. Lincoln was the Republican nominee in the 1860 presidential election. The slave states rejected his position that opposed slavery's extension into new territories but allowing it to remain in the South. Soon after his election the American Civil War started.

The war dominated Lincoln's administration. He was consumed with choosing generals, conciliating the Radical Republicans and coordinating the Union's military efforts through his high command. Lincoln wanted to unite the North, so he issued the Emancipation Proclamation that freed all slaves within the Confederacy. In his Gettysburg Address he spoke more of the war's purpose. Strategic battle victories turned the tide in the Union's favor. Lincoln was reelected in 1864.

In his second inaugural address, with victory in sight, he encouraged southerners to lay down their arms. He desired the building of a harmonious Union. On April 14, five days after the war ended, he was shot by John Wilkes Booth; he died the next day.

Today I leave you; I go to assume a task more difficult than that which devolved upon General Washington. Unless the great God who assisted him, shall be with and aid me, I must fail. But if the same omniscient mind, and the same Almighty arm that directed and protected him, shall guide and support me, I shall not fail, I shall succeed.

Let us all pray that the God of our fathers may not forsake us now. To Him I commend you all—permit me to ask that with equal sincerity and faith, you all will invoke His wisdom and guidance for me.

With these few words I must leave you—for how long I know not. Friends, one and all, I must now bid you an affectionate farewell.

(February 12, 1861 Lincoln's departure for Washington, DC)

A Proclamation—On Prayer and Fasting by Abraham Lincoln, President of the United States of America on April 30, 1863

"...It is the duty of nations as well as of men to own their dependence upon the overruling power of God; to confess their sins and transgressions in humble sorrow, yet with assured hope that genuine repentance will lead to mercy and pardon; and to recognize the sublime truth, announced in the Holy Scriptures and proven by all history, that those nations only are blessed whose God is the Lord.

...We have been recipients of the choicest bounties of Heaven. We have been preserved, these many years, in peace and prosperity. We have grown in numbers, wealth, and power as no other nation has ever grown; but we have forgotten God.

We have forgotten the gracious hand which preserved us in peace, and multiplied and enriched and strengthened us; and we have vainly imagined, in the deceitfulness of our hearts, that all these blessings were produced by some superior wisdom and virtue of our own. Intoxicated with unbroken success, we have become too self-sufficient to feel the necessity of redeeming and preserving grace, too proud to pray to the God that made us:.

It behooves us, then, to humble ourselves before the offended Power, to confess our national sins, and to pray for clemency and forgiveness:

Now, therefore, in compliance with the request, and fully concurring in the views, of the Senate, I do by this my proclamation designate and set apart Thursday, the 30th day of April, 1863, as a day of national humiliation, fasting, and prayer. And I do hereby request all the people to abstain

Abraham Lincoln (1861–1865)

on that day from their ordinary secular pursuits, and to unite at their several places of public worship and their respective homes in keeping the day holy to the Lord, and devoted to the humble discharge of the religious duties proper to that solemn occasion.

All this being done in sincerity and truth, let us then rest humbly in the hope authorized by the divine teachings, that the united cry of the nation will be heard on high, and answered with blessings no less than the pardon of our national sins, and the restoration of our now divided and suffering country of its former happy condition of unity and peace."

Abraham Lincoln on offense:

Each looked for an easier triumph, and a result less fundamental and astounding. Both read the same Bible and pray to the same God, and each invokes His aid against the other. It may seem strange that any men should dare to ask a just God's assistance in wringing their bread from the sweat of other men's faces, but let us judge not, that we be not judged. The prayers of both could not be answered. That of neither has been answered fully. The Almighty has His own purposes. 'Woe unto the world because of offenses; for it must needs be that offenses come, but woe to that man by whom the offense cometh.' "

(Inaugural Address, March 4, 1865)

Abraham Lincoln on destiny:

"I do consider that I have ever accomplished anything without God: and if it is His will that I must die by the hand of an assassin, I must be resigned. I must do my duty as I see it, and leave the rest to God."

On sewing the Almighty:

"I am exceedingly anxious that this Union, the Constitution, and the liberties of the people shall be perpetuated in accordance with the original idea for which that struggle was made, and I shall be most happy indeed if I shall be an humble instrument in the hands of the Almighty, and of this, His almost chosen people, for perpetuating the object of that great struggle."

Andrew Johnson

Religious background: No formal affiliation

A ndrew Johnson was born in Raleigh, North Carolina in 1808. He was self educated, and worked initially as a tailor and owned his own business. He married Eliza McCardle, and spent his early adult participating in debates at the local academy.

Elected a state legislator in 1835, he then went on to serve in the United States House of Representatives as governor of Tennessee. When he was elected to the United States Senate in 1857, he made a job of opposing antislavery agitation. During the Civil War, he was the only Southern senator who refused to join the Confederacy. In 1864, Johnson was selected to run for vice president with President Abraham Lincoln; he assumed the presidency after Lincoln's assassination.

During Reconstruction, the rebuilding of the South, he took a moderate stance and supported a policy that readmitted former Confederate states to the Union with few provisions for reform or civil rights for freedmen.

In March 1867, the radical Republicans created their own plan of Reconstruction: they placed the southern states under military rule, and the put restrictions on the president. Johnson was accused of violating one of these rules, and the House responded by impeaching the president for the first time in United States history. Johnson was tried by the Senate in the spring of 1868 and acquitted by one vote. Johnson remained in office until 1869, but his effectiveness had ended. He returned to Tennessee, where he won reelection to the Senate shortly before he died in 1875.

To express gratitude to God in the name of the people for the preservation of the United States is my first duty in addressing you.

(Address upon the death of Abraham Lincoln)

Let us look forward to the time when we can take the flag of our country and nail it below the Cross, and there let it wave as it waved in the olden times, and let us gather around it and inscribe for our motto: 'Liberty and Union, one and inseparable, now and forever,' and exclaim: Christ first, our country next!

I have performed my duty to God, my country, and my family. I have nothing to fear in approaching death. To me it is the mere shadow of God's protecting wing ...Here I will rest in quiet and peace beyond the reach of calumny's poisoned shaft, the influence of envy and jealous enemies, where treason and traitors or State backsliders and hypocrites in church can have no peace.

Ulysses Grant

Religious background: Methodist

United States general and 18th president of the U.S, Ulysses S. Grant was born in 1822 in Point Picasant, Ohio. His father was an Ohio tanner. Grant was educated at the military academy at West Point and fought under General Zachary Taylor in the Mexican War.

After the war, he worked at farming in Missouri and in his father's leather business. It was not a happy time for him. In the American Civil War of 1861, President Lincoln appointed him a brigadier general; it was his ability and leadership that were largely responsible for the Union victory.

He had a successful Republican presidential campaign in 1868, and was elected at the age of 46, the youngest man yet elected as president. His term in office struggled along, and involved scandal among the members of his cabinet. However, Grant did have some success with his foreign affairs as he supported civil rights for blacks, amnesty for confederate leaders, and a diversion of the currency crisis in 1874.

After retiring from the Presidency, he moved to New York. When a partner defrauded an investment firm co-owned by his son, the family was faced with poverty and debt beyond paying. In order to raise funds, Grant began writing his memoirs. He was soon diagnosed with throat cancer and he died soon after completing his writings in 1885. Mark Twain posthumously published the book, which earned a reported $450,000 in royalties for Grant's family.

In conclusion I ask patient forbearance one toward another throughout the land, and a determined effort on the part of every citizen to do his share toward cementing a happy union; and I ask the prayers of the nation to Almighty God in behalf of this consummation.

(First Inaugural Address, March 4, 1869)

I believe in the Holy Scriptures, and whoso lives by them will be benefited thereby. Men may differ as to the interpretation, which is human, but the Scriptures are man's best guide. Yes, I know, and I feel very grateful to the Christian people of the land for their prayers in my behalf. There is no sect or religion, as shown in the Old or New Testament, to which this does not apply.

God gave us Lincoln and liberty. Let's fight for both.

Rutherford B. Hayes

Religious background: No formal affiliation

Rutherford B. Hayes was born in Delaware, Ohio. Educated at Harvard Law School, Hayes became an accomplished Whig lawyer. He represented defendants in fugitive-slave cases, and soon was aligned with the new Republican Party.

Hayes fought in the Union army, and then went on to sit in the U.S. House of Representatives from 1865–67. As the governor of Ohio, he supported the currency, advocating that it be backed with gold.

In 1876 he won the Republican nomination for president. During the election there were questions about the electoral vote, so a special Electoral Commission awarded the election to Hayes. Hayes brought dignity and honesty to the presidency, and his wife, Lucy Webb Hayes, promptly banished liquor and wine from the White House. The president wanted to protect blacks in the south, yet he also compromised by withdrawing federal troops from the South, which pleased the southerners. This resulted in the end of Reconstruction.

During his administration he supported civil service reform, and he used federal troops against strikers in the railroad strikes of 1877. At the end of his term, he announced that he would not serve a second term. He retired to Ohio and continued to work for humanitarian causes. He died in 1893.

O Lord our Heavenly Father, who has safely brought us to the beginning of this day; defend us in the same with Thy Almighty power. Grant that we may not fall into any kind of danger and keep us from evil. May all our doings be ordered by Thy governance so that all we do may be righteous in Thy sight. Amen.

(President and Mrs. Hayes said this prayer with their family every morning. Mrs. Hayes brought morning prayer to the White House. On Sunday evenings, cabinet members and congressmen joined in the Sunday evening hymn singing with the President and his wife.)

Rutherford Hayes on justice, peace and union:

"Looking for the guidance of that Divine Hand by which the destinies of nations and individuals are shaped, I call upon you, Senators, Representatives, judges, fellow-citizens, here and everywhere, to unite with me in an earnest effort to secure to our country the blessings, not only of material prosperity, but of justice, peace, and union—a union depending not upon the constraint of force, but upon the loving devotion of a free people; and that all things may be so ordered and settled upon the best and surest foundations that peace and happiness, truth and justice, religion and piety, may be established among us for all generations."

(Inaugural Address, March 5, 1877)

On Jesus Christ:

"I am a firm believer in the Divine teachings, perfect example, and atoning sacrifice of Jesus Christ. I believe also in the Holy Scriptures as the revealed word of God to the world for its enlightenment and salvation."

James Garfield

Religious background: Disciples of Christ

James A. Garfield was known as the "last of the log cabin presidents." He was born in Cuyahoga County, Ohio, in 1831. Fatherless, he paid his way through school and supported himself. He graduated from Williams College in 1856. Garfield then became a professor and ultimately the president of Western Reserve Eclectic Institute, which later became Hiram College.

He was elected to the Ohio Senate in 1859, and then led a brigade at Middle Creek, Kentucky in 1862. He moved up the military ladder, and then was elected to Congress. He resigned his commission on advice from President Lincoln, and was soon the leading Republican in the House. Garfield became a "dark horse" nominee for president at the 1880 convention and won the presidency by a small margin.

Garfield's administration was successful in many areas. Domestically, he strengthened Federal authority over the New York Customs House. In foreign affairs, the administration sought to hold a conference, during 1882, of American republics in Washington. But the conference never took place. The president was shot and mortally wounded in a Washington railroad station in 1881 by a mentally unbalanced attorney who had been turned down for a consular post. In an attempt to save him,

Alexander Graham Bell tried to extract the bullet with an induction-balance electrical device that he had designed. Unfortunately, he failed, and Garfield was taken to the New Jersey seaside. He seemed to improve, but took a sudden turn and died on September 19, 1881, from an infection and internal bleeding.

Public outrage and grief over Garfield's death focused immediate and passionate support for his programs of civil service. So, his term, although shortened, was punctuated by success.

I shall greatly rely upon the wisdom and patriotism of Congress and of those who may share with me the responsibilities and duties of administration, and, above all, upon our efforts to promote the welfare of this great people and their Government. I reverently invoke the support and blessings of Almighty God.

(Inaugural Address, March 4, 1881)

James Garfield on slavery:

"My countrymen, we do not now differ in our judgment concerning the controversies of past generations, and fifty years hence our children will not be divided in their opinions concerning our controversies. They will surely bless their fathers and their fathers' God that the Union was preserved, that slavery was overthrown, and that both races were made equal before the law. Above all, upon our efforts to promote the welfare of this great people and their Government I reverently invoke the support and blessings of Almighty God."

On God's reign:

"Fellow citizens, God reigns and the government at Washington still lives."

Chester Arthur

Religious background:
Episcopalian

Chester Arthur was born in N. Fairfield, Vermont. He practiced law in New York City from 1854. He became active in local Republican politics. During his early career he was appointed Customs Collector for the Port of New York.

In 1880 at the Republican National Convention, Arthur became the compromise choice for vice president on the ticket with J. Garfield. After Garfield's assassination, Arthur became president.

Chester Arthur was a man of fashion in his garb and associates, and often was seen with the elite of Washington, New York, and Newport. Republicans were angered when President Arthur, the onetime Collector of the Port of New York became a champion of civil service reform, but the public pressure after Garfield's assassination forced congress to heed Arthur.

The Arthur Administration is known for enacting the first general Federal immigration law, making illegal the immigration of criminals, paupers, and mentally ill people. Arthur demonstrated as President that he was above factions within the Republican Party, if indeed not above the party itself. It is thought that his reason was a secret he kept: he was suffering from a fatal kidney disease. He ran for president in 1884 so as to appear that he didn't fear defeat or failure, but was not re-nominated, and died in 1886. Publisher Alexander K. McClure recalled, "No man ever entered the Presidency so profoundly and widely distrusted, and no one ever retired ... more generally respected."

It has long been the pious custom of our people, with the closing of the year, to look back upon the blessings brought to them in the changing course of the seasons and to return solemn thanks to the All-Giving Source from whom they flow.

(Thanksgiving, 1881)

A Proclamation—Thanksgiving Day 1881 by Chester A. Arthur, President of the United States of America

It has long been the pious custom of our people, with the closing of the year, to look back upon the blessings brought to them in the changing course of the seasons and to return solemn thanks to the all-giving source from whom they flow.

And although at this period, when the falling leaf admonishes us that the time of our sacred duty is at hand, our nation still lies in the shadow of a great bereavement, and the mourning which has filled our hearts still finds its sorrowful expression toward the God before whom we but lately bowed in grief and supplication, yet the countless benefits which have showered upon us during the past twelve-month call for our fervent gratitude and make it fitting that we should rejoice with thankfulness that the Lord in His infinite mercy has most signally favored our country and our people.

Peace without and prosperity within have been vouchsafed to us, no pestilence has visited our shores, the abundant privileges of freedom which our fathers left us in their wisdom are still our increasing heritage; and if in parts of our vast domain sore affliction has visited our brethren in their forest homes, yet even this calamity has been tempered and in a manner sanctified by the generous compassion for the sufferers which has been called forth throughout our land. For all these things it is meet that the voice of the nation should go up to God in devout homage.

Wherefore, I, Chester A. Arthur, President of the United States, do recommend that all the people observe Thursday, the 24th day of November instant, as a day of national thanksgiving and prayer, by

Chester Arthur (1881–1885)

ceasing, so far as may be, from their secular labors and meeting in their several places of worship, there to join in ascribing honor and praise to Almighty God, whose goodness has been so manifest in our history and in our lives, and offering earnest prayers that His bounties may continue to us and to our children.

In witness whereof I have hereunto set my hand and caused the seal of the United States to be affixed.

Done at the city of Washington, this 4th day of November, A.D. 1881, and of the Independence of the United States of America the one hundred and sixth.

Chester A. Arthur

Grover Cleveland

Religious background: Presbyterian

Grover Cleveland was the first Democrat elected after the Civil war, and the only President to leave the White House and then complete a second term four years later. He was the 22nd and 24th president of the United States

He was born in Caldwell, New Jersey, and practiced law in Buffalo, New York. In 1859, he entered Democratic Party politics. As the mayor of Buffalo, he was known as an enemy of corruption. He also served as governor of New York City, where he faced with the anger of Tammany Hall due to his independence. Yet, in 1884, he won the Democratic nomination for president. In June 1886, Cleveland married Frances Folsom becoming the only president married while in the White House. As president, he supported civil-service reform and opposed high protective tariffs, which became an issue in the 1888 election, when Benjamin Harrison narrowly defeated him. Although he won the popular majority, he had less electoral votes.

In 1892 he was reelected by a huge popular vote. In his second term, he faced acute economic depression, yet he was able to deal with the Treasury crisis, farm mortgage foreclosures and unemployment. In 1893, he attributed the United States' severe economic depression to the

Sherman Silver Purchase Act of 1890 and strongly urged Congress to repeal the act. All of this economic unrest resulted in the Pullman Strike in 1894.

Because he was an isolationist, Cleveland opposed territorial expansion. So, in 1895 he invoked the Monroe Doctrine in the border dispute between Britain and Venezuela. His policies during the depression were not popular, and his party left him and nominated William Jennings Bryan in 1896. Cleveland retired to New Jersey, where he lectured at Princeton University. He died in 1908.

And let us not trust in human effort alone, but humbly acknowledge the power and goodness of Almighty God, who presides over the destiny of nations, and who has at all times been revealed in our country's history; let us invoke His aid and His blessings upon our labors.

(Inaugural Address, March 4, 1885)

Above all, I know there is a Supreme Being who rules the affairs of men and whose goodness and mercy have always followed the American people, and I know He will not turn from us now if we humbly and reverently seek His powerful aid.

(2nd Inaugural Address, March 4, 1893)

Grover Cleveland on the teachings of Christ:

"All must admit that the reception of the teachings of Christ results in the purest patriotism, in the most scrupulous fidelity to public trust, and in the best type of citizenship. Those who manage the affairs of government are by this means reminded that the law of God demands that they should be courageously true to the interests of the people, and that the Ruler of the Universe will require of them a strict account of their stewardship. The teachings of both human and Divine law thus merging into one word, duty, form the only union of Church and state that a civil and religious government can recognize."

On blessing:

"Unto God's gracious care we commit thee. The Lord bless and keep thee. The Lord make his face to shine upon thee and be gracious unto thee and give thee peace now, and forever more. Amen."

(From Numbers 6:22–26, requested by Grover Cleveland of Rev. Will Cleveland when Cleveland married Francis Folsom.)

Benjamin Harrison

Religious background: Presbyterian

Benjamin Harrison was born in 1833 on a farm outside of Cincinnati, Ohio. He studied at Miami University in Ohio. After getting his law degree, Harrison moved to Indianapolis. There he practiced law and campaigned for the Republican Party. He married Caroline Lavinia Scott in 1853. His grandfather, William Henry Harrison, was the ninth president.

After the Civil War, he became prominent in Indianapolis, and was thought of as brilliant. He served in the United States Senate from 1881–87. Nominated for President, Harrison held one of the first "front-porch" campaigns, where he gave short speeches to delegations that visited him in Indianapolis. He was only 5 feet, 6 inches tall, so disdainful Democrats nicknamed him "Little Ben."

Harrison was nominated for president in 1889 by the Republicans. He defeated the incumbent, Grover Cleveland, even though Cleveland won more of the popular vote than Harrison.

As president, his domestic policy was marked by passage of the Sherman Antitrust Act. His foreign policy expanded United States influence abroad and he was proud of his accomplishments in that area. At the end of his

Benjamin Harrison (1889–1893)

administration Harrison submitted to the Senate a treaty to annex Hawaii. To his disappointment, President Cleveland later withdrew it.

Harrison's party re-nominated him in 1892, but he was defeated for reelection by Cleveland. Harrison returned to Indianapolis to practice law, and from 1898 to 1899 he was the leading counsel for Venezuela in its boundary dispute with Britain. He married the widowed Mrs. Mary Dimmick in 1896, and in 1901, he died as a dignified statesman.

My promise is spoken; yours unspoken, but not the less real and solemn... Entering thus solemnly into covenant with each other, we may reverently invoke and confidently expect the favor and help of Almighty God—that He will give to me wisdom, strength, and fidelity, and to our people a spirit of fraternity and a love of righteousness and peace.

(Inaugural Address, March 4, 1889)

Benjamin Harrison on Christian people:

"The importance for man and beast of the prescribed weekly rest, the sacred rights of Christian soldiers and sailors, a becoming deference to the best sentiment of a Christian people, and a due regard for the divine will demand that Sunday labor in the Army and Navy be reduced to the measure of strict necessity."

"No other people have a government more worthy of their respect and love or a land so magnificent in extent, so pleasant to look upon, and so full of generous suggestion to enterprise and labor. God has placed upon our head a diadem and has laid at our feet power and wealth beyond definition or calculation. But we must not forget that we take these gifts upon the condition that justice and mercy shall hold the reins of power and that the upward avenues of hope shall be free to all the people."

William McKinley

Religious background: Methodist

William McKinley was born in Niles, Ohio in 1843. As a young adult, he briefly attended Allegheny College, and was teaching school when the Civil War broke out. He enlisted in the Union Army. Afterwards, he studied law and opened an office in Canton, Ohio, where he married Ida Saxton.

He was elected to the United States House of Representatives, where he sponsored the McKinley Tariff of 1890 which established high rates that protected tariffs and helped stabilize the economy recovering from economic depression. His intelligence, pleasing personality and fine character helped him attain his goals. He was elected governor in 1892, and in 1896 he won the Republican presidential nomination and the general election, defeating W. J. Bryan.

Foreign policy dominated his administration. McKinley called a special session of Congress to increase customs duties, but was soon involved in events in Cuba and the sinking of the USS Maine, which led to the Spanish-American War.

At the war's end, Cuba had established independence from Spain and McKinley advocated United States dependency status for the Philippines,

Puerto Rico, and other former Spanish territories. He ran against Bryan again in 1900, and defeated him. His second term began well, but came to a tragic end in September 1901. While standing in a receiving line at the Buffalo Pan-American Exposition, he was fatally shot by an anarchist. Eight days later, he died from his wounds.

Let me again repeat the words of the oath administered by the Chief Justice which, in their respective spheres, so far as applicable, I would have all my countrymen observe: "I will faithfully execute the office of President of the United States, and will, to the best of my ability, preserve, protect, and defend the Constitution of the United States". This is the obligation I have reverently taken before the Lord Most High. To keep it will be my single purpose, my constant prayer; and I shall confidently rely upon the forbearance and assistance of all the people in the discharge of my solemn responsibilities.

(1st Inaugural Address, March 4, 1897)

William McKinley on following Christ:

"There is no currency in this world that passes at such a premium anywhere as good Christian character. The time has gone by when the young man or the young woman in the United States has to apologize for being a follower of Christ. No cause but one could have brought together so many people, and that is the cause of our Master."

On obeying God's commandments:

"Our faith teaches that there is no safer reliance than upon the God of our fathers, who has so singularly favored the American people in every national trial, and who will not forsake us so long as we obey His commandments and walk humbly in His footsteps."

On God's guidance:

"Entrusted by the people for a second time with the office of President, I enter upon its administration appreciating the great responsibilities which attach to this renewed honor and commission, promising unreserved devotion on my part to their faithful discharge and reverently invoking for my guidance the direction and favor of Almighty God."

Theodore Roosevelt

Religious background: Dutch Reformed

In 1958, Theodore Roosevelt was born into a prominent, wealthy family in New York. Despite health issues, he was able to triumph throughout his career. He was elected to the New York legislature in 1882. His wife and mother died the same day. Soon after, while visiting London, he met and married Edith Carow.

Roosevelt returned to New York and there held office in the United States Civil Service Commission, and then led the city's board of police commissioners. He served as an assistant secretary of the Navy. When the Spanish-American War was declared, he resigned to organize a cavalry unit, the Rough Riders.

Back again in New York, Roosevelt was hailed a hero, and was elected governor in 1899. He then became the Republican vice-presidential nominee, and took office when McKinley was reelected. Theodore Roosevelt became president when McKinley was assassinated in 1901.

While President, Roosevelt believed that the Government should help put economic conflicts to an end within the nation. His favorite proverb was, "Speak softly and carry a big stick." Some of Roosevelt's accomplishments included the regulation of railroads, the passing of the Pure Food and Drug Act and Meat Inspection Act, as well as making huge strides in conservation. He was awarded the Nobel peace Prize in 1906 for assisting with the end of the Russo-Japanese War. And Roosevelt also managed to secure a treaty with Panama for construction of a trans-isthmus canal.

He declined seeking reelection and instead traveled Africa and Europe. He organized the Bull Moose Party and ran again for president in 1912, but lost. He wrote extensively. He was shot by a "fanatic" while on campaign, yet recovered. He died quietly in 1919.

No people on earth have more cause to be thankful than ours, and this is said reverently, in no spirit of boastfulness in our own strength, but with the gratitude to the Giver of good who has blessed us.

(Inaugural Address, March 4, 1905)

A Proclamation - Thanksgiving Day 1907 by Theodore Roosevelt, President of the United States of America

Once again the season of the year has come when, in accordance with the custom of our forefathers for generations past, the president appoints a day as the special occasion for all our people to give praise and thanksgiving to God.

During the past year we have been free from famine, from pestilence, from war. We are at peace with all the rest of mankind. Our natural resources are at least as great as those of any other nation. We believe that in ability to develop and take advantage of these resources the average man of this nation stands at least as high as the average man of any other. Nowhere else in the world is there such an opportunity for a free people to develop to the fullest extent all its powers of body, of mind, and of that which stands above both body and mind—character.

Much has been given us from on high, and much will rightly be expected of us in return. Into our care the ten talents have been entrusted; and we are to be pardoned neither if we squander and waste them, nor yet if we hide them in a napkin; for they must be fruitful in our hands. Ever throughout the ages, at all times and among all peoples, prosperity has been fraught with danger, and it behooves us to beseech the Giver of all things that we may not fall into lose of ease and luxury; that we may not lose our sense of moral responsibility; that we may not forget our duty to God, and to our neighbor.

A great democracy like ours, a democracy based upon the principles of orderly liberty, can be perpetuated only if in the heart of ordinary citizens there dwells a keen sense of righteousness, and justice. We should

Theodore Roosevelt (1901–1909)

earnestly pray that this spirit of righteousness and justice may grow in the hearts of all of us, and that our souls may be inclined ever more both toward the virtues that tell for gentleness and tenderness, for loving kindness and forbearance, one toward another, and toward those no less necessary virtues that make for manliness and rugged hardihood; for without these qualities neither nation nor individual can rise to the level of greatness.

Now, therefore, I, Theodore Roosevelt, President of the United States, do set apart Thursday, the 28th day of November, as a day for general Thanksgiving and Prayer, and on that day I recommend that the people shall cease from their daily work, and in their homes or in their churches, meet devoutly to thank the Almighty for the many and great blessings they have received in the past, and to pray that they may be given the strength so to order their lives as to deserve a continuation of these blessings in the future.

In witness whereof I have hereunto set my hand and caused the seal of the United States to be affixed.

Done at the city of Washington, this the 26th day of October in the year of our Lord, 1907, and of the Independence of the United States, the 132nd.

Theodore Roosevelt

William Taft

Religious background: Unitarian

William Taft was a large, jovial man who was known for his effectiveness as an administrator, but also for his failures at being a successful politician.

In 1857, Taft was born in Cincinnati, Ohio. He was the son of a prominent judge, and as a young adult he graduated from Yale and practiced law in Cincinnati. He was able to acquire Republican judiciary appointments easily and served in many offices including the state superior court, as United States Solicitor General in Benjamin Harrison's administration and as United States appellate judge. He was then appointed head of the Philippine Commission in 1901 and became its first civilian governor.

Under President Roosevelt, Taft served as United States Secretary of War in 1904, and Roosevelt in turn supported Taft's nomination for president in 1908, even though Taft clearly preferred law to politics. Although Taft won the presidential election, his affiliation with conservative Republicans cause problems with party progressives, which in turn caused a split with Roosevelt and his Bull Moose Party. This prevented Taft's reelection.

After leaving office, Taft taught law at Yale University, served on the National War Labor Board, and supported the League of Nations. He then became Chief Justice of the United States Supreme Court, which he held as the greatest honor of his lifetime. He worked toward making that office more efficient. At his resignation in 1930, he was in poor health. He died shortly after leaving his much-loved job as Chief Justice.

I invoke the considerate sympathy and support of my fellow-citizens and the aid of the Almighty God in the discharge of my responsible duties.

(Inaugural Address, March 4, 1909)

No man can study the movement of modern civilization from an impartial standpoint, and not realize that Christianity and the spread of Christianity are the basis of hope of modern civilization in the growth of popular self government. The spirit of Christianity is pure democracy. It is equality of man before God—the equality of man before the law, which is, as I understand it, the most God-like manifestation that man has been able to make.

A Proclamation—Thanksgiving Day 1909 by William H. Taft, President of the United States of America

The season of the year has returned when, in accordance with the reverent custom established by our forefathers, the people of the United States are wont to meet in their usual places of worship on a day of thanksgiving appointed by the civil magistrate, to return thanks to God for the great mercies and benefits which they have enjoyed.

During this past year we have been highly blessed. No great calamities of flood or tempest or epidemic sickness have befallen us.

We have lived in quietness, undisturbed by wars or rumors of war. Peace and the plenty of bounteous crops and of great industrial production animate a cheerful and resolute people to all the renewed energies of beneficent industry and material and moral progress.

It is altogether fitting that we should humbly and gratefully acknowledge the divine source of these blessings.

Therefore, I hereby appoint Thursday, the 25th day of November, as a day of general Thanksgiving. And I call upon the people on that day, laying aside their usual vocations, to repair to their churches and unite in appropriate services of praise and thanks to Almighty God.

In witness whereof I have hereunto set my hand and caused the seal of the United States to be affixed.

Done at the city of Washington, this 15th day of November in the year of our Lord one thousand nine hundred and nine, and of the independence of the United States the one hundred and thirty-fourth.

William H. Taft

Woodrow Wilson

Religious background: Presbyterian

Woodrow Wilson was born in Virginia in 1856, the son of a Presbyterian minister. From Johns Hopkins University he earned a law degree and a doctorate. As a professor he taught at Princeton University and became its president in 1902.

Wilson had the support of the progressives who helped him gain the office of governor of New Jersey in 1910, and then as the Democratic presidential nominee in 1912. His campaign was called "New Freedom" and led to his overwhelming electoral win of the presidency.

As president, he approved legislation that lowered tariffs, created the Federal Reserve System, established the Federal Trade Commission, and strengthened labor unions. In foreign affairs he promoted self-government for the Philippines and sought to contain the Mexican civil war. From 1914 he maintained United States neutrality in World War I, offering to mediate a settlement and initiate peace negotiations.

His second campaign was based on the idea that Wilson had "kept us out of war." He was reelected in 1916, and asked for a declaration of war shortly after in April of 1917. His desire for peace led him to write the Fourteen Points in 1918, and he traveled to the Paris Peace Conference to stand on his principles. When Wilson presented to the Senate the Versailles Treaty, which contained the Covenant of the League of Nations, it was defeated by the Republican Senate. The president, in bad health, made a national tour to gain awareness and support for the treaty. This tour led to his exhaustion and an eventual stroke, which nearly cause his death. His wife, Edith Bolling Galt, nursed Wilson until his death in 1924.

> *I pray God I may be given the wisdom and prudence to do my duty in the true spirit of this great people.*
>
> *(2nd Inaugural Address, March 5, 1917)*

Woodrow Wilson on the Bible:

"A nation which does not remember what it was yesterday, does not know what it is today, nor what it is trying to do. We are trying to do a futile thing if we do not know where we came from or what we have been about.....

"The Bible is the one supreme source of revelation of the meaning of life, the nature of God, and spiritual nature and needs of men.

"It is the only guide of life which really leads the spirit in the way of peace and salvation. America was born a Christian nation.

"America was born to exemplify that devotion to the elements of righteousness which are derived from the revelations of Holy Scripture.

"I have a very simple thing to ask of you. I ask every man and woman in this audience that from this day on they will realize that part of the destiny of America lies in their daily perusal of this great Book (the Bible)."

On justice and mercy:

"The Nation has been deeply stirred, stirred by a solemn passion, stirred by the knowledge of wrong, of ideals lost, of government too often debauched and made an instrument of evil. The feelings with which we face this new age of right and opportunity sweep across our heartstrings like some air out of God's own presence, where justice and mercy are reconciled and the judge and the brother are one."

(1st Inaugural Address,
March 4, 1913)

Warren Harding

Religious background: Baptist

W arren Harding was born near Marion, Ohio, in 1865, and in adulthood became the publisher of a newspaper. He married a divorcee, Mrs. Florence Kling De Wolfe.

Harding was a prominent man, and was a member of many clubs and organizations during his early career. He became part of the Republican political machine, serving as an Ohio state senator, a lieutenant governor, and as a United States senator. He was highly conservative, and was chosen at the Republican convention of 1920 as the compromise candidate for president.

Harding promised a "return to normalcy" after World War I, and consequently won the election of 1920. The Republicans in Congress were able to eliminate wartime controls and slash taxes, as well as complete a budget, restore protective tariffs, and tighten immigration. But Harding's administration was flawed by corruption. His Secretary of the Interior took bribes from oil companies in exchange for allowing them to drill for oil on federal land in California and Teapot Dome, Wyoming.

Depressed and uncertain, Harding was afraid to publicly expose the scandals and corruption, and went against the advice of Hoover by not doing so. He did not live long enough to know the full repercussions of the scandal, because he died suddenly of a heart attack in August of 1923.

I have taken the solemn oath of office on that passage of Holy Writ wherein it is asked: "What doth the Lord require of thee but to do justly, and to love mercy, and to walk humbly with thy God?" This I plight to God and country.

(Inaugural Address, March 4, 1921)

A Proclamation—Thanksgiving Day 1921 by Warren G. Harding, President of the United States of America

That season has come when, alike in pursuance of a devout people's time-honored custom and in grateful recognition of favoring national fortunes, it is proper that the President should summon the nation to a day of devotion, of thanksgiving for blessings bestowed, and of prayer for guidance in modes of life that may deserve continuance of Divine favor.

Foremost among our blessings is the return of peace, and the approach to normal ways again. The year has brought us again into relations of amity with all nations, after a long period of struggle and turbulence. In thankfulness therefore, we may well unite in the hope that Providence will vouchsafe approval to the things we have done, the aims which have guided us, the aspirations which have inspired us.

We shall be prospered as we shall deserve prosperity, seeking not alone for the material things but for those of the spirit as well; earnestly trying to help others; asking, before all else, the privilege of service. As we render thanks anew for the exaltation which came to us, we may fittingly petition that moderation and wisdom shall be granted to rest upon all who are in authority, in the tasks they must discharge. Their hands will be steadied, their purposes strengthened, in answer to our prayers.

Ours has been a favored nation in the bounty which God has bestowed upon it. The great trial of humanity, though indeed we bore our part as well as we were able, left us comparatively little scarred. It is for us to recognize that we have been thus favored, and when we gather at our altars to offer up thanks, we will do well to pledge, in humility and all sincerity, our purpose to prove deserving.

Warren G. Harding (1912–1923)

We have been raised up and preserved in national power and consequence, as part of a plan whose wisdom we can not question. Thus believing, we can do no less than hold our nation the willing instrument of the Providence which has so wonderfully favored us. Opportunity for very great service awaits us if we shall prove equal to it. Let our prayers be raised, for direction in the right paths. Under God, our responsibility is great; to our own first, to all men afterward; to all mankind in God's own justice.

Now, therefore, I, Warren G. Harding, President of the United States of America, hereby designate Thursday, the twenty-fourth day of November, to be observed by the people as a day of Thanksgiving, devotion and prayer; urging that at their hearthsides and their altars they will give thanks for all that has been rendered unto them, and will pray for a continuance of the Divine fortune which has been showered so generously upon this nation.

In witness whereof, I have hereunto set my hand and caused the seal of the United States to be affixed.

Done at the City of Washington this thirty-first day of October in the year of our Lord, one thousand nine hundred and twenty-one, and of the independence of the United States OF America the one hundred and forty-sixth.

Warren G. Harding

Calvin Coolidge

Religious background:
Congregationalist

Calvin Coolidge was born in 1872 in Vermont, but it was in Massachusetts that he was educated and climbed the political ladder to Governor of Massachusetts. He was a conservative republican. Nicknamed "Silent Cal", in 1920 he was nominated for vice president on Warren G. Harding's winning ticket. When Harding died in office in 1923, Coolidge became president.

The Harding administration had been full of scandal, and Coolidge brought a feeling of trustworthiness back to the office. As a result, he won the presidential election in 1924.

America was prosperous during this time, and Coolidge attempted to keep the old economic moral by vetoing measures to provide farm relief and bonuses to World War I veterans. His dry wit and frugality with words are remembered to this day, and his most memorable short statement was, "I do not choose to run for President in 1928."

Coolidge is remembered for his conservative policies of domestic and international inaction, and these policies are symbols of the era between World War I and the Great Depression. By the time Great Depression was

Calvin Coolidge (1923–1929)

in full swing, Coolidge was retired. Alfred E. Smith believed that Coolidge's "great(est) task was to restore the dignity and prestige of the Presidency when it had reached the lowest ebb in our history ... in a time of extravagance and waste...." Coolidge died in January of 1933.

Here stands our country, an example of tranquility at home, a patron of tranquility abroad. Here stands its Government, aware of its might but obedient to its conscience. Here it will continue to stand, seeking peace and prosperity, solicitous for the welfare of the wage earner, promoting enterprise, developing waterways and natural resources, attentive to the intuitive counsel of womanhood, encouraging education, desiring the advancement of religion, supporting the cause of justice and honor among the nations. America seeks no earthly empire built on blood and force. No ambition, no temptation, lures her to thought of foreign dominions. The legions which she sends forth are armed, not with the sword, but with the cross. The higher state to which she seeks the allegiance of all mankind is not of human, but of divine origin. She cherishes no purpose save to merit the favor of Almighty God.

(Inaugural Address, March 1, 1925)

Calvin Coolidge on working in harmony with Divine Providence:

"The Government of the United States has been created by the people. It is solely responsible to them. It will be most successful if it is conducted solely for their benefit. All its efforts would be of little avail unless they brought more justice, more enlightenment, more happiness and prosperity into the home. This means an opportunity to observe religion, secure education, and earn a living under a reign of law and order. It is the growth and improvement of the material and spiritual life of the Nation. We shall not be able to gain these ends merely by our own action. If they come at all, it will be because we have been willing to work in harmony with the abiding purpose of a Divine Providence."

(Written message to Congress, December 8, 1925)

On faith:

"Our country has been provided with the resources with which it can enlarge its intellectual, moral, and spiritual life. The issue is in the hands of the people. Our faith in man and God is the justification for the belief in our continuing success."

(Annual Message to Congress, December 4, 1928)

On the rule of God:

"There is in the soul of the nation a reserve for responding to the call to high ideals, to nobility of action, which has never yet been put forth. There is no problem so great but that somewhere a man is being raised up to meet it. There is no moral standard so high that the people cannot be raised up to it. God rules, and from the Bethlehems and the Springfields He sends them forth, His own, to do His work. In them we catch a larger gleam of the Infinite."

(Coolidge speech on "The Place of Lincoln," February 12, 1922)

Calvin Coolidge on contemplating what God has done:

"It is not only through action, but through contemplation that people come to understand themselves. Man does not live by bread alone. This thought is expressed in the motto of the sanctuary in the words of John Burroughs: 'I come here to find myself. It is so easy to get lost in the world.' We are so thickly crowded with the forest of events that there is not only danger that we can not see the trees, but that we may lose our sense of direction. Under the influence of these beautiful surroundings we can pause unhampered while we find out where we are and whither we are going. Those who come here report the feeling of peace which they have experienced. In the expression of an ancient writer, it is a place to which to invite one's soul, where one may see in the landscape and foliage, not what man has done, but what God has done."

(The Bok Tower Address, February 1, 1929)

Calvin Coolidge on spirit versus materialism:

"No other theory is adequate to explain or comprehend the Declaration of Independence. It is the product of the spiritual insight of the people. We live in an age of science and of abounding accumulation of material things. These did not create our Declaration. Our Declaration created them. The things of the spirit come first. Unless we cling to that, all our material prosperity, overwhelming though it may appear, will turn to a barren scepter in our grasp. If we are to maintain the great heritage which has been bequeathed to us, we must be like minded as the fathers who created it. We must not sink into a pagan materialism. We must cultivate the reverence which they had for the things that are holy. We must follow the spiritual and moral leadership which they showed. We must keep replenished, that they may glow with a more compelling flame, the altar fires before which they worshipped."

(Speech on "The Inspiration of the
Declaration of Independence," July 5, 1926)

On reverence for God's name:

"More than six centuries ago, when in spite of much learning and much piety there was much ignorance, much wickedness and much warfare, when there seemed to be too little light in the world, when the condition of the common people appeared to be sunk in hopelessness, when most of life was rude, harsh and cruel, when the speech of men was too often profane and vulgar, until the earth rang with the tumult of those who took the name of the Lord in vain, the foundation of this day was laid in the formation of the Holy Name Society. It had an inspired purpose. It sought to rededicate the minds of the people to a true conception of the sacredness of the name of the Supreme Being. It was an effort to save all reference to the Deity from curses and blasphemy, and restore the lips of men to reverence and praise. Out of weakness there began to be strength;

out of frenzy there began to be self-control; out of confusion there began to be order. This demonstration is a manifestation of the wide extent to which an effort to do the right thing will reach when it is once begun. It is a purpose which makes a universal appeal, an effort in which all may unite.

The importance of the lesson which this Society was formed to teach would be hard to overestimate. Its main purpose is to impress upon the people the necessity for reverence. This is the beginning of a proper conception of ourselves, of our relationship to each other, and our relationship to our Creator. Human nature cannot develop very far without it. The mind does not unfold, the creative faculty does not mature, the spirit does not expand, save under the influence of reverence. It is the chief motive of an obedience. It is only by a correct attitude of mind begun early in youth and carried through maturity that these desired results are likely to be secured. It is along the path of reverence and obedience that the race has reached the goal of freedom, of self-government, of a higher morality, and a more abundant spiritual life."

(Address delivered to The Holy Name
Society, September 21, 1924)

Herbert Hoover

Religious background: Society of Friends (Quaker)

Herbert Hoover grew up in Oregon after he was born in Branch, Iowa. He attended Stanford University at its opening in 1891, and after graduation became a mining engineer. He married his Stanford sweetheart, Lou Henry, and then became responsible for engineering projects on four continents. Afterwards, he was in charge of Allied relief projects in Europe. During World War I, Hoover was appointed United States national food administrator, and he initiated programs to feed areas of starving Europe. As the United States secretary of commerce in 1921, he worked towards organizing regulation of broadcasting and aviation divisions

He became the Republican presidential candidate in 1928 and won the election. His hopes for his administration, what he called the "New Day" program, were not possible due to problems caused by the Great Depression and the crash of the stock market. Hoover believed in individual rights and freedoms, and because of these beliefs, he vetoed bills to create a federal unemployment agency and to fund public-works projects. In 1932 he approved relief to farmers through the Reconstruction Finance Corporation.

Herbert Hoover (1929–1933)

Hoover was blamed for the Depression, and portrayed by Congress to be a cruel, uncaring president. Though badly defeated in the 1932 election, Hoover continued to speak out against relief measures and criticized New Deal programs. After World War II he participated in famine-relief work in Europe and was appointed head of the Hoover Commission. Hoover left a legacy as President as someone who was reputable for public service as an engineer, administrator, and humanitarian. Hoover wrote many articles, essays and books, and actively writing when he died in 1964.

This occasion is not alone the administration of the most sacred oath which can be assumed by an American citizen. It is a dedication and consecration under God to the highest office in service of our people. I assume this trust in the humility of knowledge that only through the guidance of Almighty Providence can I hope to discharge its ever-increasing burdens.... In the presence of my countrymen, mindful of the solemnity of this occasion, knowing what the task means and the responsibility which it involves, I beg your tolerance, your aid, and your cooperation. I ask the help of Almighty God in this service to my country to which you have called me.

(Inaugural Address, March 4, 1929)

Herbert Hoover on the Bible:

"Menaced by collectivist trends, we must seek revival of our strength in the spiritual foundations which are the bedrock of our republic. Democracy is the outgrowth of the religious conviction of the sacredness of every human life. On the religious side, its highest embodiment is the Bible; on the political side, the Constitution."

Herbert Hoover on prayer:

"There are only two occasions when Americans respect privacy especially in presidents. Those are prayer and fishing."

A Proclamation—Thanksgiving Day 1929 by Herbert Hoover, President of the United States of America

At this season of the year, when the harvest had been gathered in, the thoughts of our forefathers turned toward God with thanksgiving for the blessings of plenty and provision against the needs of winter. They came by custom to look to the Chief Magistrate to set apart a day of prayer and praise whereon their thanks as a united people might be given with one voice in unison. God has greatly blessed us as a nation in the year now drawing to a close. The earth has yielded an abundant harvest in most parts of our country. The fruits of industry have been of unexampled quantity and value. Both capital and labor have enjoyed an exceptional prosperity.

Assurances of peace, at home and abroad, have been strengthened and enlarged. Progress has been made in provision against preventable disasters from flood and pestilence. Enlightenment has grown apace in new revelations of scientific truth and in diffusion of knowledge. Educational opportunities have steadily enlarged. Enduring advances have been gained in the protection of the public health. Childhood is measurably more secure. New experience and new knowledge in many fields have been recorded, from which a deeper wisdom may grow. We should accept these blessings with resolution to devote them to service of Almighty God.

Now, therefore, I, Herbert Hoover, President of the United States of America, do appoint and set aside Thursday, the twenty-eighth day of November, as a day of National Thanksgiving, and do recommend that all our people on that day rest from their daily work that they should extend to others less fortunately placed, a share in their abundance, and that they gather at their accustomed places of worship, there to render up thanks to Almighty God for His many blessings upon them, for his forbearance and goodness.

In witness whereof, I have hereunto set my hand and caused to be affixed the great seal of the United States.

Done at the City of Washington, this 5th day of November, in the year of our Lord One Thousand Nine Hundred and Twenty-nine, and of the Independence of the United States, the One Hundred and Fifty-fourth.

Herbert Hoover

Franklin D. Roosevelt

Religious background: Episcopal

Franklin D. Roosevelt, a distant cousin of Theodore Roosevelt, was born in Hyde Park, New York, he became active in the Democratic Party after attending university at both Harvard and Columbia. In 1905 he married Eleanor Roosevelt, who was his valued advisor as well as beloved wife. In his early career, he served in the state senate, and as United States Assistant Secretary of the Navy.

In 1920 he was nominated for vice president. At the age of 39, he was stricken with polio that rendered him unable to walk, although he continued to swim and work at using his legs. Polio did not deter him from politics.

He became governor of New York in 1928, and went on to win the Democratic nomination in 1932. His inaugural address contained the famous words, "...the only thing we have to fear is fear itself." Congress passed most of the changes he sought in his New Deal program in the first hundred days of his term. Roosevelt had programs of reform that included Social Security.

In an unprecedented move, Roosevelt was reelected to a third term, and maintained a neutral stance toward the war in Europe. After the bombing of Pearl Harbor in 1941, Roosevelt organized America for war.

Franklin D. Roosevelt (1933–1945)

Roosevelt felt that peace would come with good relations between the United States and Russia, and he spent a large amount of time planning the United Nations. He was reelected to a fourth term in 1944. As World War II drew to a close, Roosevelt's health began to fail. On April 12, 1945, while at Warm Springs, Georgia, he died of a cerebral hemorrhage.

Franklin Roosevelt's D-Day Prayer

June 6, 1944

My fellow Americans: Last night, when I spoke with you about the fall of Rome, I knew at that moment that troops of the United States and our allies were crossing the Channel in another and greater operation. It has come to pass with success thus far. And so, in this poignant hour, I ask you to join with me in prayer:

Almighty God: Our sons, pride of our Nation, this day have set upon a mighty endeavor, a struggle to preserve our Republic, our religion, and our civilization, and to set free a suffering humanity.

Lead them straight and true; give strength to their arms, stoutness to their hearts, steadfastness in their faith.

They will need Thy blessings. Their road will be long and hard. For the enemy is strong. He may hurl back our forces. Success may not come with rushing speed, but we shall return again and again; and we know that by Thy grace, and by the righteousness of our cause, our sons will triumph.

They will be sore tried, by night and by day, without rest-until the victory is won. The darkness will be rent by noise and flame. Men's souls will be shaken with the violences of war.

For these men are lately drawn from the ways of peace. They fight not for the lust of conquest. They fight to end conquest. They fight to liberate. They fight to let justice arise, and tolerance and good will among all Thy people. They yearn but for the end of battle, for their return to the haven of home.

Some will never return. Embrace these, Father, and receive them, Thy heroic servants, into Thy kingdom.

And for us at home—fathers, mothers, children, wives, sisters, and brothers of brave men overseas—whose thoughts and prayers are ever with them—help us, Almighty God, to rededicate ourselves in renewed faith in Thee in this hour of great sacrifice.

Many people have urged that I call the Nation into a single day of special prayer. But because the road is long and the desire is great, I ask that our people devote themselves in a continuance of prayer. As we rise to each new day, and again when each day is spent, let words of prayer be on our lips, invoking Thy help to our efforts.

Give us strength, too—strength in our daily tasks, to redouble the contributions we make in the physical and the material support of our armed forces.

And let our hearts be stout, to wait out the long travail, to bear sorrows that may come, to impart our courage unto our sons wheresoever they may be.

And, O Lord, give us Faith. Give us Faith in Thee; Faith in our sons; Faith in each other; Faith in our united crusade. Let not the keenness of our spirit ever be dulled. Let not the

Franklin D. Roosevelt (1933–1945)

impacts of temporay events, of temporal matters of but fleeting moment let not these deter us in our unconquerable purpose.

With Thy blessing, we shall prevail over the unholy forces of our enemy. Help us to conquer the apostles of greed and racial arrogancies. Lead us to the saving of our country, and with our sister Nations into a world unity that will spell a sure peace a peace invulnerable to the schemings of unworthy men. And a peace that will let all of men live in freedom, reaping the just rewards of their honest toil.

Thy will be done, Almighty God. Amen.

Franklin D. Roosevelt on peace:

"So we pray to Him now for the vision to see our way clearly... to the achievement of His will, to peace on earth."

On the Bible:

"We cannot read the history of our rise and development as a nation, without reckoning with the place the Bible has occupied in shaping the advances of the Republic. Where we have been the truest and most consistent in obeying its precepts, we have attained the greatest measure of contentment and prosperity."

Harry Truman

Religious background: Baptist

Harry S. Truman was born and raised in western Missouri into a hardworking farm family. He worked as a bank clerk and on the family farm until he was thirty years old. Truman finally left the farm in 1914 when his father died. He tried his hand at different business ventures, but failed. In 1918, Truman became a field officer in World War I. He served overseas and became a war hero. On his arrival home he married Bess Wallace became a shopkeeper in Kansas City and later entered politics.

At the Democratic National Convention in 1944, he was selected to be President Roosevelt's running mate. The Roosevelt-Truman ticket was victorious in 1944. After winning the 1944 election and only 82 days as vice president, Truman became president when Roosevelt died in 1945.

As president, Truman immediately arranged the charter-writing meeting of the United Nations, worked on Germany's unconditional surrender that ended World War II in Europe and in July attended the Potsdam Conference. The Pacific war ended after his military orders were issued dropping atomic bombs on Hiroshima and Nagasaki.

Truman also established the Truman Doctrine, he established the Central Intelligence Agency, and urged the passage of the Marshall Plan. In 1948 he won reelection. He retired to Independence, Missouri and died at the age of 88.

At this moment, I have in my heart a prayer. As I have assumed my heavy duties, I humbly pray, Almighty God, in the words of King Solomon: "Give therefore thy servant an understanding heart to judge thy people, that I may discern between good and bad: for who is able to judge this thy so great a people?" I ask only to be a good and faithful servant of my Lord and my people.

(Address to Congress, April 16, 1945)

Oh! Almighty and Everlasting God, Creator of Heaven, Earth and the Universe, help me to be, to think, to act what is right, because it is right; make me truthful, honest and honorable in all things; make me intellectually honest for the sake of right and honor and without thought of reward to me. Give me the ability to be charitable, forgiving and patient with my fellowmen—help me to understand their motives and their short-coming—even as Thou understandest mine! Amen, Amen, Amen.

According to President Truman: "The prayer on this page has been said by me—by Harry S. Truman—from high school days, as a window washer, bottle duster, floor scrubber in an Independence, Mo., drugstore, as a time-keeper on a railroad contract gang, as an employee of a newspaper, as a bank clerk, as a farmer riding a gang plow behind four horses and mules, as a fraternity official learning to say nothing at all if good could not be said of a man, as public official judging the weaknesses and shortcomings of constituents, and as President of the United States of America."

(August 15, 1950. On record
at the Truman Presidential
Museum and Library)

33rd President of the United States

Harry Truman on faith:

"The American people stand firm in the faith which has inspired this Nation from the beginning. We believe that all men have a right to equal justice under law and equal opportunity to share in the common good. We believe that all men have the right to freedom of thought and expression. We believe that all men are created equal because they are created in the image of God. From this faith we will not be moved.... Steadfast in our faith in the Almighty, we will advance toward a world where man's freedom is secure. To that end we will devote our strength, our resources, and our firmness of resolve. With God's help, the future of mankind will be assured in a world of justice, harmony, and peace."

(Inaugural Address, January 20, 1949)

On biblical morality:

"The fundamental basis of this nation's laws was given to Moses on the Mount. The fundamental basis of our Bill of Rights comes from the teachings we get from Exodus and Saint Matthew, from Isaiah and Saint Paul. I don't think we emphasize that enough these days. If we don't have a proper fundamental moral background, we will finally end up with a totalitarian government which does not believe in rights for anybody except the State!"

On God's help in victory:

"Our global victory has come from the courage and stamina and spirit of free men and women united in determination to fight. It has come from the massive strength of arms and materials created by peace-loving peoples who knew that unless they won decency in the world would end. It has come from millions of peaceful citizens all over the world-turned soldiers almost overnight—who showed a ruthless enemy that they were not afraid to fight and to die, and that they knew how to win. It has come with the help of God, Who was with us in the early days of adversity and disaster, and Who has now brought us to this glorious day of triumph. Let us give thanks to Him, and remember that we have now dedicated ourselves to follow in His ways to a lasting and just peace and to a better world."

(Victory in the East-Day of Prayer, August 16, 1945)

Dwight D. Eisenhower

Religious background: Presbyterian

Born in Texas in 1890, Eisenhower had six brothers. As a young adult, he went into West Point. While stationed in Texas he met Mamie Geneva Doud, whom he married in 1916. In his early army career he excelled as a supreme commander in the Pacific war. After the war, Eisenhower became president of Columbia University.

He took his leave of Columbia in 1951 and became supreme commander over NATO forces; soon after he was persuaded to run for president by supporters in 1952. His campaign slogan was, "I like Ike," and Eisenhower won a huge victory.

While in office "Ike" worked to reduce the stress of the cold war. The creation of the hydrogen bomb caused much tension and Eisenhower proposed at the Geneva Convention of 1955 that the United States and Russia exchange blueprints of each other's military establishments. The Russians were not agreeable, but tensions did begin to relax at the convention. Eisenhower suddenly suffered a heart attack in September of 1955. He recovered and ran for a second term in November, which he won.

Eisenhower impacted the balancing of the budget by continuing most of the New Deal and Fair Deal programs, and also played a part in the desegregation of schools by sending troops into Little Rock, Arkansas, to assure compliance. Eisenhower also commanded the complete desegregation of the armed forces, stating, "There must be no second class citizens in this country." He also continued his focus on world peace throughout his administration.

He left office in 1961 and went to his farm in Gettysburg. He died after a long illness in March of 1969.

Almighty God, as we stand here, at this moment, my future associates in the executive branch of the government join me in beseeching that Thou will make full and complete our dedication to the service of the people in this throng and their fellow citizens everywhere. Give us, we pray, the power to discern clearly right from wrong and allow all our works and actions to be governed thereby and by the laws of the land. Especially we pray that our concerns shall be for all the people, regardless of station, race, or calling. May cooperation be permitted and be the mutual aim of those who, under the concept of our Constitution, hold to differing political beliefs, so that all may work for the good of our beloved country and for Thy glory. Amen.

(2nd Inaugural Address, Jan. 21, 1957)

Dwight Eisenhower on the Bible:

"The spirit of man is more important than mere physical strength, and the spiritual fiber of a nation than its wealth. The Bible is endorsed by the ages. Our civilization is built upon its words. In no other book is there such a collection of inspired wisdom, reality, and hope."

Dwight D. Eisenhower (1953–1961)

On right from wrong:

"Give us, we pray, the power to discern clearly right from wrong, and allow all of our words and actions to be governed thereby...Especially we pray that our concern shall be for all the people regardless of station, race or calling."

John F. Kennedy

Religious background: Roman Catholic

John Fitzgerald Kennedy was born in Brookline, Massachusetts, on May 29, 1917. He graduated from Harvard University in 1940, and then entered the Navy. In 1943, when his PT boat was rammed and sunk by a Japanese destroyer, Kennedy, despite his injuries, led the survivors to safety. Elected to the United States House of Representatives and Senate, he supported social legislation and became increasingly committed to civil rights legislation.

He married Jacqueline Bouvier on September 12, 1953. In 1955, while recuperating from a back operation, he wrote *Profiles in Courage*, which won the Pulitzer Prize in history.

In 1960 he won the Democratic nomination for president; after a vigorous campaign, managed by his brother Robert Kennedy and aided financially by his father, he narrowly defeated Richard M. Nixon. He was the youngest person and the first Roman Catholic elected president.

In his inaugural address he called on Americans to "ask not what your country can do for you, ask what you can do for your country." In office, he proposed tax-reform and civil-rights legislation, but received little congressional support. Kennedy also established the Peace Corps and the Alliance for Progress.

His foreign policy began with the abortive Bay of Pigs invasion of Cuba in 1961. In 1963 he successfully concluded the Nuclear Test-Ban Treaty.

In November 1963 he was assassinated while riding in a motorcade in Dallas by a sniper. Kennedy's youth, energy, humor, and idealism made him a charismatic figure worldwide. Kennedy was not only the youngest man elected President; he was also the youngest to die while in office.

And so, my fellow Americans: ask not what your country can do for you—ask what you can do for your country. My fellow citizens of the world: ask not what America will do for you, but what together we can do for the freedom of man.

Finally, whether you are citizens of America or citizens of the world, ask of us the same high standards of strength and sacrifice which we ask of you. With a good conscience our only sure reward, with history the final judge of our deeds, let us go forth to lead the land we love, asking His blessing and His help, but knowing that here on earth God's work must truly be our own.

(Inaugural Address, January 20, 1961)

A Proclamation—Thanksgiving Day 1963 by John F. Kennedy, President of the United States of America

Let us therefore proclaim our gratitude to Providence for manifold blessings — let us be humbly thankful for inherited ideals — and let us resolve to share those blessings and those ideals with our fellow human beings throughout the world.

NOW, THEREFORE, I, JOHN F KENNEDY, President of the United States of America, in consonance with the joint resolution of the Congress approved December 26, 1941, 55 Stat. 862 (5 U.S>C. 87b), designating the fourth Thursday of November in each year as Thanksgiving Day, do hereby proclaim Thursday, November 28, 1963, as a day of national thanksgiving.

On that day let us gather in sanctuaries dedicated to worship and in homes blessed by family affection to express our gratitude for the glorious gifts of God; and let us earnestly and humbly pray that He will continue to guide and sustain us in the great unfinished tasks of achieving peace, justice, and understanding among all men and nations and of ending misery and suffering wherever they exist.

(Thanksgiving Proclamation)

John F. Kennedy (1961–1963)

On prayer:

"Do not pray for easy lives. Pray to be stronger men."

On keeping watch:

"We in this country, in this generation are, by destiny rather than choice, the watchmen on the walls of world freedom. We ask, therefore, that we may be worthy of our power and responsibility, that we may exercise our strength with wisdom and restraint, and that we may achieve in our time and for all time the ancient vision of peace on earth, goodwill toward men. That must always be our goal. For as was written long ago, 'Except the Lord keep the city, the watchman waketh but in vain.'"

Lyndon Johnson

Religious background: Disciples of Christ

L yndon Johnson was born on Aug. 27, 1908 near Johnson City, Texas. On Nov. 17, 1934, he married Claudia Alta Taylor, known as "Lady Bird." A warm, intelligent, ambitious woman, she was a great asset to Johnson's career. In 1937, Johnson sought and won a Texas seat in Congress, where he championed public works, reclamation, and public power programs. In 1948 he ran for the United States Senate, winning the Democratic Party's primary by only 87 votes. The opposition accused him of fraud and derisively tagged him "Landslide Lyndon." Although challenged, unsuccessfully, in the courts, he took office in 1949.

In the late 1950s, Johnson began to think seriously of running for the presidency in 1960. The presidential nomination of 1960 went to Senator John F. Kennedy of Massachusetts. Kennedy selected Johnson as his running mate. In November 1960 the Democrats defeated the Republican candidates by a narrow margin.

Johnson was appointed by Kennedy to head the President's Committee on Equal Employment Opportunities, a post that enabled him to work on behalf of blacks and other minorities. As vice-president, he also undertook some missions abroad, which offered him some limited insights into international problems.

Lyndon Johnson (1963–1969)

Lyndon Baines Johnson became the 36th president of the United States on the assassination of John F. Kennedy in November 1963. Easily re-elected in 1964, LBJ was able to pass sweeping social legislation including the Civil Rights Act, Medicare, and the Voting Rights Act. His decision to escalate American involvement in Vietnam, however, proved to be extremely unpopular. This decision eroded his popular standing and led to his decision not to run for reelection to the presidency in 1968.

After leaving office in 1969, Johnson returned to his ranch in Texas. There he wrote his memoirs, which were published in 1971. He also supervised construction of the Johnson Presidential Library in Austin. Johnson died on January 22, 1973, five days before the treaty of withdrawal from Vietnam was concluded.

If we fail now, we will have forgotten that democracy rests on faith.... For myself, I ask only in the words of an ancient leader: "Give me now wisdom and knowledge that I may go out and come in before this people."... Come now, let us reason together."

(Inaugural Address, January 20, 1965)

A Proclamation—Thanksgiving Day 1968 by Lyndon B. Johnson, President of the United States of America

Americans, looking back on the tumultuous events of 1968, may be more inclined to ask God's mercy and guidance than to offer Him thanks for his blessings.

There are many events in this year that deserve our remembrance, and give us cause for thanksgiving:

- the endurance and stability of our democracy, as we prepare once more for an orderly transition of authority;

- the renewed determination, on the part of millions of Americans to bridge our divisions;

- the beginning of talks with our adversaries, that will, we pray, lead to peace in Vietnam;

- the increasing prosperity of our people, including those who were denied any share in America's blessings in the past;

- the achievement of new breakthroughs in medical science, and new victories over disease.

These events inspire not only the deepest gratitude, but confidence that our nation, the beneficiary of good fortune beyond that of any nation in history, will surmount its present trials and achieve a more just society for its people.

In this season, let us offer more than words of thanksgiving to God. Let us resolve to offer Him the best that is within us—tolerance, respect for life, faith in the destiny of all men to live in peace.

Lyndon Johnson (1963–1969)

NOW, THEREFORE, I, LYNDON B. JOHNSON, President of the United States of America, in consonance with Section 6103 of title 5 of the United States Code designating the fourth Thursday of November in each year as Thanksgiving Day, do hereby proclaim Thursday, November 28, 1968 as a day of national thanksgiving.

IN WITNESS WHEREOF, I have hereunto set my hand this fifteenth day of November, in the year of our Lord nineteen hundred and sixty-eight, and of the Independence of the United States of America the one hundred and ninety-third.

Lyndon B. Johnson

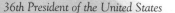

Richard M. Nixon

Religious background: Society of Friends (Quaker)

Born in California in 1913, Richard M. Nixon was an accomplished student in his youth, and went on to practice law after graduating from Duke University. He married Patricia Ryan in 1940, and served in the Navy in the Pacific. After leaving service, he served in Congress, then in the Senate. Eisenhower selected Nixon to be his running partner in 1952, and they won the election. He was nominated in 1960 for president but lost. Again in 1968 he was nominated, and this time defeating Hubert Humphrey, he began his administration.

He accomplished much while in office: revenue sharing, anticrime law making, and environmental programs to name a few. Americans first landed on the moon during his term. He also won acclaim for his quest for world stability that was successful in many arenas. Again in 1972, he won the election against George McGovern by one of the widest margins in history.

Soon Nixon's administration was marred by scandal. The "Watergate" scandal stemmed from a break-in at the Democratic offices in the Watergate Apartment complex. Nixon tried to divert the investigations and was tried and found out. As a result, the vice president, Spiro Agnew, resigned and was replace by Gerald Ford. Faced with impeachment, Nixon announced his resignation on August 8, 1974. He believed it would lead to healing in America.

In Nixon's last years of life, he spent time writing his memoirs and books on foreign policy, and was regarded as an elder statesman. He died in April of 1994.

Let us go forward, firm in our faith, steadfast in our purpose, cautious of the dangers; but sustained by our confidence in the will of God and the promise of man.

(1st Inaugural Address, January 20, 1969)

Today, I ask your prayers that in the years ahead I may have God's help in making decisions that are right for America, and I pray for your help so that together we may be worthy of our challenge. Let us go forward from here confident in hope, strong in our faith in one another, sustained by our faith in God who created us, and striving always to serve His purpose.

(2nd Inaugural Address, January 20th, 1973)

A Proclamation—Thanksgiving Day 1969 by Richard M. Nixon, President of the United States of America

On October 3, 1863, President Abraham Lincoln invited his fellow citizens to "set apart and observe the last Thursday of November next as a day of Thanksgiving..." This was the year of the battle of Gettysburg and of other major battles between Americans on American soil. To many, this call for a national day of Thanksgiving must have seemed strange, coming as it did at a time of war and bitterness.

Yet Lincoln knew that the act of thanksgiving should not be limited to time of peace and serenity. He knew that it is precisely at those times of hardship when men most need to recognize that the Source of all good constantly bestows His blessings on mankind.

Today, despite our material wealth and well-being, Americans face complex problems unknown before in our nation's history. In giving thanks today, we express gratitude for past bounty and we also confidently face the challenges confronting our own nation and the world because we know we can rely on a strength greater than ourselves.

This year, let us especially seek to rekindle in our respective hearts and minds the spirit of our first settlers who valued freedom above all else, and who found much for which to be thankful when material comforts were meager. We are, indeed, a most fortunate people.

Richard Milhous Nixon (1969–1974)

NOW, THEREFORE, I, RICHARD NIXON, President of the United States of America, in consonance with Section 6103 of Title 5 of the United States Code designating the fourth Thursday of November in each year as Thanksgiving Day, do hereby proclaim Thursday, November 27, 1969, as a day of national thanksgiving.

IN WITNESS WHEREOF, I have hereunto set my hand this twelfth day of November, in the year of our Lord nineteen hundred sixty-nine, and of the Independence of the United States of America the one hundred ninety-fourth.

Richard Nixon

Gerald Ford

Religious background: Episcopal

Gerald R. Ford was the first vice president chosen under the terms of the Twenty-fifth Amendment. It was after the Watergate scandal that he became the successor to the first president ever to resign.

He was born in Omaha, Nebraska, in 1913, and he lived in Grand Rapids, Michigan. He attended Yale University where he earned his law degree. Ford served as a lieutenant commander in the Navy during the war, and afterwards practiced law. In 1948 he married Elizabeth Bloomer and was elected to Congress shortly afterwards. His honesty and strong character made him popular while in Congress. It was from there that he became House Minority Leader. Soon after, he became the 38th president of the United States upon the resignation of Richard M. Nixon.

While in office, Ford faced many obstacles and difficult tasks. Inflation, economic problems and energy shortages troubled the nation. Ford worked hard to curb Government intervention and excessive spending. He also granted a pardon to former President Nixon. Ford held the office of president for 14 months, and he viewed himself as a "a moderate in domestic affairs, a conservative in fiscal affairs, and a dyed-in-the-wool internationalist in foreign affairs."

Gerald Ford (1974–1977)

President Ford won the Republican nomination for the Presidency in 1976, but lost the election. He was thanked in President Jimmy Carter's inaugural speech for healing the Nation during his time as president.

May God guide this wonderful country, its people, and those they have chosen to lead them. May our third century be illuminated by liberty and blessed with brotherhood, so that we and all who come after us may be the humble servants of thy peace. Amen.

(State of the Union Address, Jan. 12, 1977)

Gerald Ford on God:

"Without God there could be no American form of government, nor an American way of life. Recognition of the Supreme Being is the first—the most basic—expression of Americanism. Thus, the founding fathers of America saw it, and thus with God's help, it will continue to be."

On doing what's right with God:

"Mr. Speaker, I am not discouraged. I am indeed humble to be the 40th Vice President of the United States, but I am proud — very proud — to be one of 200 million Americans. I promise my fellow citizens only this: To uphold the Constitution, to do what is right as God gives me to see the right, and within the limited powers and duties of the Vice Presidency to do the very best that I can for America."

(Dec. 6, 1973 to Joint Session of Congress)

On praying for Richard Nixon:

"In the beginning, I asked you to pray for me. Before closing, I ask again your prayers, for Richard Nixon and for his family. May our former President, who brought peace to millions, find it for himself. May God bless and comfort his wonderful wife and daughters, whose love and loyalty will forever be a shining legacy to all who bear the lonely burdens of the White House."

(Aug. 9, 1974 after taking the oath of office.)

On praying for blessing:

"For my part I pray the third century we are beginning will bring to all Americans, our children and their children's children, a greater measure of individual equality, opportunity, and justice, a greater abundance of spiritual and material blessings, and a higher quality of life, liberty, and the pursuit of happiness."

(State of the Union Address, Jan. 12, 1977)

Jimmy Carter

Religious background: Baptist

J ames Earl Carter, Jr. was born October 1, 1924, in Plains, Georgia. He rarely used his whole name, and grew up on a peanut farm. He was from a Baptist family who spoke about politics in the home. Upon his graduation from the Naval Academy in 1946, he married his sweetheart, Rosalynn Smith.

He started in state politics in 1962, then became Governor of Georgia in 1968. He emphasized ecology, government efficiency, and racial equality. Carter began his campaign for President in December 1974, and at the Democratic Convention, he gained the nomination immediately. He won the election by a small margin against Gerald Ford.

As president, Carter helped negotiate a peace treaty between Egypt and Israel, signed a treaty with Panama to make the Panama Canal a neutral zone after 1999, and established full diplomatic relations with China. He dealt with the Iran hostage crisis and it became a major political liability for him. After facing more foreign policy problems, his administration became hampered by high inflation and a recession, all of which hit the nation. Consequently, he lost his bid for reelection to Ronald Reagan in 1980.

Carter continued to negotiate over the hostages until Iran finally released them the same day that Carter left office. After the presidency, he became an international diplomat, and became a strong advocate of democracy in nations where there is none.

Here before me is the Bible used in the inauguration of our first president in 1789, and I have just taken the oath of office on the Bible my mother gave me just a few years ago, opened to a timeless admonition from the ancient prophet Micah: "He has showed thee, O man, what is good; and what doth the lord require of thee, but to do justly, and to love mercy, and to walk humbly with thy God" (Micah 6:8).

(Inaugural Address, January 20, 1977)

I would like to have my frequent prayer answered that God let my life be meaningful in the enhancement of His kingdom and that my life might be meaningful in the enhancement of the lives of my fellow human beings.

A Proclamation—Thanksgiving Day 1980 by Jimmy Carter, President of the United States of America

"I call upon all the people of our Nation to give thanks on that day for the blessings Almighty God has bestowed upon us, and to join the fervent prayer of George Washington who as President asked God to '... impart all the blessings we possess, or ask for ourselves to the whole family of mankind.'"

(Thanksgiving Proclamation, November 27, 1980)

On Christ:

"The unchanging principles of life predate modern times. I worship Jesus Christ, whom we Christians consider to be the Prince of Peace. As a Jew, he taught us to cross religious boundaries, in service and in love. He repeatedly reached out and embraced Roman conquerors, other Gentiles, and even the more despised Samaritans."

(Nobel Prize Speech, December 10, 2002)

On prayer:

"I prayed more when I was President than any other four years of my life. I prayed more during the year that the hostages were held than any other year that I was in office — that I would have the patience to accomplish the goals that I established at the very beginning. I had two goals. One was to preserve the integrity of my nation and not do anything to embarrass my country. And the second one was to bring every hostage home safe and free. And I asked God to help me with those commitments.

I could have launched a very popular military strike on Iran. I could have destroyed Iran — and in the process killed thousands of innocent Iranians, which would also have resulted maybe the assassination or killing of American hostages. I had advice to do that. I decided not to. And I felt — I guess I felt that God would answer my prayer. Well, I never did embarrass my nation or violated its principles. Every hostage came home — safe and free. So, my prayer was answered. God answered my prayer later than I wanted. If my prayer had been answered a week before the election of 1980, I would have been a two-term President. But I understand that God answers prayers in different ways. Sometimes He answers yes, sometimes He answers no. And sometimes He answer answers late, and sometimes He answers, 'You've got to be kidding.' I don't think there's any doubt that, had I not had religious faith, I would not have been so patient."

(PBS Interview with Jimmy Carter)

Ronald Reagan

Religious background: Disciples of Christ

In 1911, Ronald Wilson Reagan was born in Tampico, Illinois. As a youth he studied at Eureka College. He was involved in sports and school plays and was a good student. He went on to be a radio sports announcer after graduation, and from there to a contract in Hollywood in 1937. Reagan appeared in 53 films. His first marriage was to an actress, Jane Wyman, with whom he had two children. In 1952 he married Nancy Davis, also an actress. They also had two children.

In the film industry, Reagan ran into problems with the issues of Communism in the industry. He became conservative and began speaking on conservatism. He became governor of California in 1966 and was reelected in 1970.

In 1980 Reagan gained the Republican Presidential nomination in 1980 and chose George Bush as his running mate. Reagan won by sweeping 489 electoral votes in 1981. He took office, and only 69 days after doing so, had an attempt made on his life when he was shot. He was quick to recover and did so with humor and gracefulness. His popularity was unquestionable.

In office, Reagan stimulated economic growth, increased employment, and worked to strengthen national defenses. Reagan and Bush won a second term in 1984. Reagan set to work and overhauled the income tax code, and his time in office reigned over peace and prosperity in the nation. Reagan sought for peace in foreign policy, and negotiated a treaty to eliminate inter-mediate-range nuclear weapons. He also declared war against terrorism.

Reagan left office in 1989, and in 1994 revealed that he was suffering from Alzheimer's disease.

To preserve our blessed land we must look to God...It is time to realize that we need God more than He needs us... We also have His promise that we could take to heart with regard to our country, that 'If my people, which are called by my name shall humble themselves, and pray and seek my face, and turn form their wicked ways; then will I hear from heaven and will forgive their sin, and will heal their land.

Let us, young and old, join together, as did the First Continental Congress, in the first step, humble heartfelt prayer. Let us do so for the love of God and His great goodness, in search of His guidance, and the grace of repentance, in seeking His blessings, His peace, and the resting of His kind and holy hands on ourselves, our nation, our friends in the defense of freedom, and all mankind, now and always.

The time has come to turn to God and reassert our trust in Him for the healing of America. . . . Our country is in need of and ready for a spiritual renewal. Today, we utter no prayer more fervently than the ancient prayer for peace on Earth.

A Proclamation—Thanksgiving Day 1982 by Ronald Reagan, President of the United States of America

Two hundred years ago, the Congress of the United States issued a Thanksgiving Proclamation stating that it was "the indispensable duty of all nations" to offer both praise and supplication to God. Above all other nations of the world, America has been especially blessed and should give special thanks. We have bountiful harvests, abundant freedoms, and a strong, compassionate people.

I have always believed that this anointed land was set apart in an uncommon way, that a divine plan placed this great continent here between the oceans to be found by people from every corner of the Earth who had a special love of faith and freedom. Our pioneers asked that He would work His will in our daily lives so America would be a land of morality, fairness, and freedom.

Today we have more to be thankful for than our pilgrim mothers and fathers who huddled on the edge of the New World that first Thanksgiving Day could ever dream. We should be grateful not only for our blessings, but for the courage and strength of our ancestors which enable us to enjoy the lives we do today.

Let us reaffirm through prayers and actions our thankfulness for America's bounty and heritage.

NOW, THEREFORE, I, RONALD REAGAN, President of the United States of America, do hereby proclaim Thursday, November 25, 1982, as a National Day of Thanksgiving and I call upon all of our citizens to set aside that day for appropriate expressions of thanksgiving.

Ronald Reagan (1981–1989)

IN WITNESS WHEREOF, I have hereunto set my hand this 27th day of Sept. in the year of our Lord nineteen hundred and eighty-two, and of the Independence of the United States of America the two hundred and seventh.

Ronald Reagan

George Bush

Religious background: Episcopal

George Herbert Walker Bush was born in Milton, Massachusetts, on June 12, 1924. He was an excellent student and academic leader, and on his 18th birthday he enlisted. He was the youngest pilot on the Navy and he flew missions throughout World War I. He was shot down during one of these missions and was later awarded the Distinguished Flying Cross for his actions in the war. After the war, Bush married Barbara Pierce in 1945 and they had six children. He attended Yale University and excelled in all areas. After he graduated he worked in the oil industry, and soon became interested in politics. He went on to serve two terms as a representative to Congress. He ran unsuccessfully for the Senate on two occasions, and then was given other important positions including Ambassador to the United Nations, Chairman of the Republican National Committee, Chief of the U. S. Liaison Office in the People's Republic of China, and Director of the Central Intelligence Agency.

Bush campaigned for president in 1980 but lost. He became vice president to Ronald Reagan, and then in 1988 Bush won the Republican nomination for President. In office Bush faced many challenges. The world was rapidly changing with the end of the cold war and the destruction of the Berlin wall. Bush worked on areas of foreign policy and sent American troops into Panama to overthrow the corrupt regime of General Manuel Noriega. Iraqi President Saddam Hussein put Bush to test over the invasion of Kuwait. Bush and the UN sent troops to implement Desert Storm, which was a 100-hour land battle.

Bush was extremely popular due to this triumph, but domestic problems like the economy and violence caused discontent and Bush lost his bid for reelection to Democrat William Clinton.

Heavenly Father, we bow our heads and thank you for Your love. Accept our thanks for the peace that yields this day and the shared faith that makes its continuance likely. Make us strong to do Your work, willing to heed and hear Your will, and write on our hearts these words: 'Use power to help people.' For we are given power not to advance our own purposes, nor to make a great show in the world, nor a name. There is but one just use of power, and it is to serve people. Help us to remember it, Lord, Amen.

A Proclamation—National Day of Prayer 1990 by George Bush, President of the United States of America

This Thanksgiving, as we enjoy the company of family and friends, let us gratefully turn our hearts to God, the loving Source of all Life and Liberty. Let us seek His forgiveness for our shortcomings and transgressions and renew our determination to remain a people worthy of His continued favor and protection. Acknowledging our dependence on the Almighty, obeying His Commandments, and reaching out to help those who do not share fully in this Nation's bounty is the most heartfelt and meaningful answer we can give to the timeless appeal of the Psalmist: "O give thanks to the Lord for He is good: for his steadfast love endures forever."

(Thanksgiving Proclamation, November 14, 1990)

George Bush on faith:

"The great faith that led our nation's founding fathers to pursue this bold experience in self-government has sustained us in uncertain and perilous times; it has given us strength and inspiration to this very day. Like them, we do very well to recall our 'firm reliance on the protection of divine providence' to give thanks for the freedom and prosperity this nation enjoys, and to pray for continued help and guidance from our wise and loving Creator."

On God's abiding presence:

"The Lord our God be with us, as He was with our fathers; may He not leave us or forsake us; so that He may incline our hearts to Him, to walk in all His ways. . . that all peoples of the earth may know that the Lord is God; there is no other."

William J. Clinton

Religious background: Baptist

President Clinton was born in 1946, in Hope, Arkansas. His father died three months later, and his mother wed Roger Clinton, of Hot Springs, Arkansas. In high school, William took the family name. He excelled as a student and musician, and desired to lead a public life from an early age. He graduated from Georgetown University and in 1968 won a Rhodes scholarship to Oxford University. He received a law degree from Yale University in 1973. Clinton entered politics in Arkansas. Clinton married Hillary Rodham, and soon after was elected Arkansas Attorney General in 1976. He then won the governorship in 1978.

In 1992, he defeated incumbent George Bush and third party candidate Ross Perot in the presidential race. This was the first time in 12 years that Democrats held both the White House and Congress. The Republicans won back the House in 1994.

Clinton was involved in a scandal in 1998 resulting from personal indiscretions with a young White House intern. This resulted in Clinton being the 2nd impeached president by the House of Representatives. He was tried and found not guilty, and then he apologized to the nation for his actions. He still proved publicly popular, and his administration had success in areas such as the expansion of NATO, more open international trade, and campaigning against drug trafficking. After he left office, he still proved to be a popular speaker, drawing huge crowds all over the world.

I try to tell everybody around the White House all the time, I have concluded a few things in my life, and one of them is that you don't ever get even. The harder you try, the more frustrated you're going to be, because nobody ever gets even. And when you do, you're not really happy. You don't feel fulfilled.

So I ask you to pray for us. I went to church last Sunday where Hillary and I always go, at the Foundry Methodist Church, and the pastor gave a sermon on Romans 12:16‑21 and a few other verses. But I'm going to quote the relevant chapters.

"Do not be wise in your own estimation." It's hard to find anybody here that can fit that. "Never pay back evil for evil to anyone." "If possible, so far, as it depends upon you, be at peace with all men." "Never take your own vengeance." "If your enemy is hungry, feed him. If he is thirsty, give him a drink" "Do not be overcome by evil, but overcome evil with good."

Pray for the people in public office that we can rid ourselves of this toxic atmosphere of cynicism, and embrace with joy and gratitude this phenomenal opportunity and responsibility before us. Do not forget people in the rest of the world who depend upon the United States for more than exhortation, and most of all, remember that in every scripture of every faith, there are hundreds and hundreds of admonitions—not forget those among us who are poor. They are no longer entitled to a handout, but they surely deserve and we are ordered to give them a hand up.

(Feb. 6, 1997, National Prayer Breakfast)

William Clinton on prayer:

"From patriots and presidents to advocates for justice, our history reflects the strong presence of prayer in American life. Presidents, above all, need the power of prayer, their own and that of all Americans. We need not shrink as Americans from asking for divine assistance in our continuing efforts to relieve human suffering at home and abroad, to reduce hatred, violence and abuse, and to restore families across our land... I encourage the citizens of this great Nation to gather, each in his or her own manner, to recognize the   blessings, acknowledge our wrongs to remember the needy, to seek guidance for our challenging future and to give thanks for the abundance we have enjoyed throughout out history."

On God's help:

"When our Founders boldly declared America's Independence to the world and our purposes to the Almighty, they knew that America, to endure, would have to change....And so, my fellow Americans, at the edge of the 21st century, let us begin with energy and hope, with faith and discipline, and let us work until our work is done. The Scripture says, 'And let us not be weary in well-doing, for in due season, we shall reap, if we faint not.' From this joyful mountaintop of celebration, we hear a call to service in the valley. We have heard the trumpets. We have changed the guard. And now, each in our way, and with God's help, we must answer the call."

(1st Inaugural Address, January 20, 1993)

A Proclamation—National Day of Prayer 1996 by William J. Clinton, President of the United States of America

America's heritage is rich with expressions of faith in God. Indeed, the desire for religious freedom was one of the chief reasons that early settlers risked their lives to come to this land. Many of those who braved the long ocean journey were men and women of devout religious beliefs who sought a new home where they might worship without persecution. The authors of our Constitution recognized this history in the language of the first amendment, and through times of uncertainty, sorrow, and pain, the citizens of the United States have called upon the wisdom and mercy of the Almighty for guidance and strength.

A National Day of Prayer, first proclaimed by the Continental Congress in 1775, stems from the understanding that faith is a fundamental part of our Nation's social fabric. In an impassioned speech before the Constitutional Convention in 1787, Benjamin Franklin put the importance of prayer in perspective, proposing that ". . . prayers imploring the assistance of Heaven, and its blessings on our deliberations, be held in this Assembly every morning before we proceed to business . . . . " And so it has been to this day in statehouses all over our great land.

Today we cherish the liberties the first immigrants fought so hard to obtain, and we enjoy a degree of freedom and prosperity only dreamed of

200 years ago. And though our citizens come from every nation on Earth and observe an extraordinary variety of religious faith and traditions, prayer remains at the heart of the American spirit. We face many of the same challenges as our forebears — ensuring the survival of freedom and sustaining faith in an often hostile world — and we continue to pray, as they did, for the blessings of a just and benevolent God to guide our Nation's course.

This occasion calls us to affirm our country's spiritual roots and to humbly express our gratitude to the source of our abundant good fortune. As we seek to renew the values that have long strengthened America's families and communities, let us reach out to God and to one another for wisdom and courage. We should celebrate this day in the tradition of our founders who believed that God governs in the affairs of men and women, and who based their greatest hopes, dreams, and aspirations on the surety of divine protection.

The Congress, by Public Law 100–307, has called on our citizens to reaffirm annually our dependence on Almighty God by recognizing a "National Day of Prayer."

NOW, THEREFORE, I, WILLIAM J. CLINTON, President of the United States of America, do hereby proclaim May 2, 1996, as a National Day of Prayer. I encourage every citizen of this great Nation to pray, each in his or her own manner, seeking strength from God to face the challenges of today, requesting guidance for the uncertainties of tomorrow, and giving thanks for the rich blessings that our Nation has enjoyed throughout our history. "Do not pray for easy lives," said John F. Kennedy in 1963, "Pray to be stronger . . . ." May it be so with each of us.

IN WITNESS WHEREOF, I have hereunto set my hand this second day of April, in the year of our Lord nineteen hundred and ninety-six, and of the Independence of the United States of America the two hundred and twentieth.

William J. Clinton

George W. Bush

Religious background: Methodist

Currently the 43rd President of the United States, George W. Bush was born on July 6, 1946, in New Haven, Connecticut. He spent his youth growing up in Texas. He graduated from Yale University in 1968, and then served in the Texas Air National Guard. He later went to business school where he received his M.A. in business in 1975. He then began a career in Energy. Bush served for six years as the 46th Governor of the State of Texas. He had an excellent reputation as a fair, compassionate, conservative governor.

In 1988, he worked on his father's campaign (George H. W. Bush.) Bush then served as managing general partner of the Texas Rangers until he was elected Governor on November 8, 1994. Bush is married to Laura Welch Bush, a former teacher and librarian, and they have twin daughters, Barbara and Jenna. George W. Bush himself ran a successful campaign years later. In 2001 he was sworn into office.

Bushes administration has affected change in many areas: he has signed initiative to improve public schools, he has signed tax relief, he has increased pay for American military personnel, and he had made Social

Security and Medicare a priority. He has also begun a "war on terror" after the September 11th attacks on America. He extended his war on terrorism with a war against the regime of Saddam Hussein in Iraq to unseat the dictator and restore freedom in Iraq.

I especially feel that because I believe in prayer. I pray. I pray for strength, I pray for guidance, I pray for forgiveness. And I pray to offer my thanks for a kind and generous Almighty God. We pray for the families that have known recent loss. We pray for the men and women who serve around the world to defend our freedom. We pray for their families. We pray for wisdom to know and do what is right. And we pray for God's peace in the affairs of men.

(National Prayer Breakfast, February 6, 2003)

George W. Bush on God's purpose:

"After the Declaration of Independence was signed, Virginia statesman John Page wrote to Thomas Jefferson: 'We know the Race is not to the swift nor the Battle to the Strong. Do you not think an Angel rides in the Whirlwind and directs this Storm?' Much time has passed since Jefferson arrived for his inaugural. The years and changes accumulate. But the themes of this day he would know: our nation's grand story of courage, and its simple dream of dignity.

"We are not this story's author, who fills time and eternity with His purpose. Yet His purpose is achieved in our duty; and our duty is fulfilled in service to one another. Never tiring, never yielding, never finishing, we renew that purpose today: to make our country more just and generous; to affirm the dignity of our lives and every life. This work continues. This story goes on. And an angel still rides in the whirlwind and directs this storm. God bless you, and God bless our country."

(Inaugural Speech, January 20, 2001)

George W. Bush (2001–?)

September 14, 2001 from the National Cathedral after the 9/11 Terrorists Attack:

On this national day of prayer and remembrance, we ask Almighty God to watch over our nation, and grant us patience and resolve in all that is to come. We pray that He will comfort and console those who now walk in sorrow. We thank Him for each life we now must mourn, and the promise of a life to come.

As we have been assured, neither death nor life, nor angels nor principalities nor powers, nor things present nor things to come, nor height nor depth, can separate us from God's love. May He bless the souls of the departed. May He comfort our own. And may He always guide our country.

God bless America.

A Proclamation—National Day of Prayer 2003 by George W. Bush, President of the United States of America

We are a Nation whose people turn to prayer in times of our most heartfelt sorrow and our moments of greatest joy. On this National Day of Prayer, first called for more than 225 years ago by the Continental Congress, we come together to thank God for our Nation's many blessings, to acknowledge our need for His wisdom and grace, and to ask Him to continue to watch over our country in the days ahead.

America welcomes individuals of all backgrounds and religions, and our citizens hold diverse beliefs. In prayer, we share the universal desire to speak and listen to our Maker and to seek the plans He has for our lives. We recognize the ways that He has blessed our land abundantly, and we offer thanks for these gifts and for the generosity of our Nation in helping those in need. We are grateful for our freedom, for God's love, mercy, and forgiveness, and for a hope that will never be shaken.

Today, our Nation is strong and prosperous. Our Armed Forces have achieved great success on the battlefield, but challenges still lie ahead. Prayer will not make our path easy, yet prayer can give us strength and hope for the journey.

As we continue to fight against terror, we ask the Almighty to protect all those who battle for freedom throughout the world and our brave men and women in uniform, and we ask Him to shield innocents from harm. We recognize the sacrifice of our military families and ask God to grant them peace and strength. We will not forget the men and women who have fallen in service to America and to the cause of freedom. We pray that their loved ones will receive God's comfort and grace.

George W. Bush (2001–?)

In this hour of history's calling, Americans are bowing humbly in churches, synagogues, temples, mosques, and in their own homes, in the presence of the Almighty. This day, I ask our Nation to join me in praying for the strength to meet the challenges before us, for the wisdom to know and do what is right, for continued determination to work towards making our society a more compassionate and decent place, and for peace in the affairs of men.

The Congress, by Public Law 100-307, as amended, has called on our citizens to reaffirm the role of prayer in our society and to honor the religious diversity our freedom permits by recognizing annually a "National Day of Prayer."

NOW, THEREFORE, I, GEORGE W. BUSH, President of the United States of America, do hereby proclaim May 1, 2003, as a National Day of Prayer. I ask the citizens of our Nation to pray, each after his or her own faith, in thanksgiving for the freedoms and blessings we have received and for God's continued guidance and protection. I also urge all Americans to join in observing this day with appropriate programs, ceremonies, and activities.

IN WITNESS WHEREOF, I have hereunto set my hand this thirtieth day of April, in the year of our Lord two thousand three, and of the Independence of the United States of America the two hundred and twenty-seventh.

George W. Bush

Prayer in the Oval Office

President Bush's Prayers
(excerpted from Judy Keen, USA Today)

After President Bush met with Macedonian President Boris Trajkovski in the White House this month, Bush invited his guest into his private study. There, the two men knelt side by side in silent prayer. White House aides didn't mention that devotional interlude when they described Trajkovski's visit May 2 to reporters, and they were displeased to learn that the private moment was about to become public.

Religion infuses the president's daily life. Bush, 54, starts every day on his knees, praying. He reads the Bible each morning and studies a daily Bible lesson. He often asks a Cabinet secretary to lead a prayer at the beginning of Cabinet meetings. He says he frequently prays in the Oval Office. He sometimes prays on the phone with a minister friend who lives in Houston.

Bush's family, friends and longtime aides say faith helped him quit drinking, find his vocation in politics and check his fiery temper. He says it has made him more humble and tolerant.

"I find great comfort in my faith," he told Fox News last month. "It helps me realize that I am a person that has a lot of responsibility, but I am just a person—nothing more than a human being who seeks redemption, solace and strength through something greater than me."

...Religion has been central to Bush's life since 1985, when he had a pivotal conversation with Rev. Billy Graham. At the time, Bush was in his late 30s, hard-partying and unfocused. He did not take his religion seriously. Graham questioned him about his commitment to his faith, Bush wrote in his autobiography, A Charge to Keep, and "planted the seed of faith in my heart. ... It was the beginning of a new walk where I would recommit my heart to Jesus Christ."

(May 18, 2001)

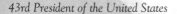

George Washington's Prayer Journal

From William J. Johnson *George Washington, the Christian* (New York: The Abingdon Press, New York & Cincinnati, 1919), pp. 24–35.

Sunday Morning...

Almighty God, and most merciful father, who didst command the children of Israel to offer a daily sacrifice to thee, that thereby they might glorify and praise thee for thy protection both night and day, receive, O Lord, my morning sacrifice which I now offer up to thee: I yield thee humble and hearty thanks that thou has preserved me from the danger of the night past, and brought me to the light of the day, and the comforts thereof, a day which is consecrated ot thine own sevice and for thine own honor. Let my heart, therefore, Gracious God, be so affected with the glory and majesty of it, that I may not do mine own works, but wait on thee, and discharge those weighty duties thou requirest of me, and since thou art a God of pure eyes, and wilt be sanctified in all who draww near unto thee, who doest not regard the sacrifice of fools, nor hear sinners who

tread in thy courts, pardon, I beseech thee, my sins, remove them from thy presence, as far as the east is from the west, and accept of me for the merits of thy son Jesus Christ, that when I come into thy temple, and compass thine altar, my prayers may come before thee as incense; and as thou wouldst hear me calling upon thee in my prayers, so give me grace to hear thee calling on me in thy word, that it may be wisdom, righteousness, reconciliation and peace to the saving of the soul in the day of the Lord Jesus. Grant that I may hear it with reverence, receive it with meekness, mingle it with faith, and that it may accomplish in me, Gracious God, the good work for which thou has sent it. Bless my family, kindred, friends and country, be our God & guide this day and for ever for his sake, who ay down in the Grave and arose again for us, Jesus Christ our Lord, Amen.

Sunday Evening...

O most Glorious God, in Jesus Christ my merciful and loving father, I acknowledge and confess my guilt, in the weak and imperfect performance of the duties of this day. I have called on thee for pardon and forgiveness of sins, but so coldly and carelessly, that my prayers are become my sin and stand in need of pardon. I have heard thy holy word, but with such deadness of spirit that I have been an unprofitable and forgetful hearer, so that, O Lord, tho' I have done thy work, yet it hath been so negligently that I may rather expect a curse than a blessing from thee. But, O God, who art rich in mercy and plenteous in redemption, mark not, I beseech thee, what I have done amiss; remember that i am but dust, and remit my transgressions, negligences & ignorances, and cover them all with the absolute obedience of thy dear Son, that those sacrifices which I have offered may be accepted by thee, in and for the sacrifice of Jesus Christ offered upon the cross for me; for his sake, ease me of the burden of my sins, and give me grace that by the call of the Gospel I may rise from the slumber of sin into the newness of life. Let me live according to those holy rules which thou hast this day prescribed in thy holy word; make me to know what is acceptable in thy holy word; make me to know what is acceptable in thy sight, and therein to delight, open the eyes of my understanding, and help me thoroughly to examine myself concerning my knowledge, faith and repentance, increase my faith, and direct me to the true object Jesus Christ the way,

the truth and the life, bless O Lord, all the people of this land, from the highest to the lowest, particularly those whom thou has appointed to rule over us in church & state. continue thy goodness to me this night. These weak petitions I humbly implore thee to hear accept and ans. for the sake of thy Dear Son Jesus Christ our Lord, Amen.

Monday Morning...

O eternal and everlasting God, I presume to present myself this morning before thy Divine majesty, beseeching thee to accept of my humble and hearty thanks, that it hath pleased thy great goodness to keep and preserve me the night past from all the dangers poor mortals are subject to, and has given me sweet and pleasant sleep, whereby I find my body refreshed and comforted for performing the duties of this day, in which I beseech thee to defend me from all perils of body and soul. Direct my thoughts, words and work, wash away my sins in the immaculate blood of the lamb, and purge my heart by thy holy spirit, from the dross of my natural corruption, that I may with more freedom of mind and liberty of will serve thee, the ever lasting God, in righteousness and holiness this day, and all the days of my life. Increase my faith in the sweet promises of the gospel; give me repentance from dead works; pardon my wanderings, & direct my thoughts unto thyself, the God of my salvation; teach me how to live in thy fear, labor in thy service, and ever to run in the ways of thy commandments; make me always watchful over my heart, that neither the terrors of conscience, the loathing of holy duties, the love of sin, nor an unwillingness to depart this life, may cast me into a spiritual slumber, but daily frame me more 7 more into the likeness of thy son Jesus Christ, that living in thy fear, and dying in thy favor, I may in thy appointed time attain the resurrection of the just unto eternal life

bless my family, friends & kindred unite us all in praising & glorifying thee in all our works begun, continued, and ended, when we shall come to make our last account before thee blessed saviour, who hath taught us thus to pray, our Father, &c.

Monday Evening...

Most Gracious Lord God, from whom proceedeth every good and perfect gift, I offer to thy divine majesty my unfeigned praise & thanksgiving for all thy mercies towards me. Thou mad'st me at first and hst ever since sustained the work of thy own hand; thou gav'st thy Son to die for me; and hast given me assurance of salvation, upon my repentance and sincerely endeavoring to conform my life to his holy precepts and example. Thou art pleased to lengthen out to me the time of repentance and to move me to it by thy spirit and by the word, by thy mercies, and by thy judgments; out of a deepness of thy mercies, and by my own unworthiness, I do appear before thee at this time; I have sinned and done very wickedly, be merciful to me, O God, and pardon me for Jesus Christ sake; instruct me in the particulars of my duty, and suffer me not to be tempted above what thou givest me strength to bear. Take care, I pray thee of my affairs and more and more direct me in thy truth, defend me from my enemies, especially my spiritual ones. Suffer me not to be drawn from thee, by the blandishments of the world, carnal desires, the cunning of the devil, or deceitfulness of sin. work in me thy good will and pleasure, and discharge my mind from all things that are displeasing to thee, of all ill will and discontent, wrath and bitterness, pride & vain conceit of myself, and render me charitable, pure, holy, patient and heavenly minded. be with me at the hour of death; dispose me for it, and

deliver me from the slavish fear of it, and make me willing and fit to die whenever thou shalt call me hence. Bless our rulers in church and state. bless O Lord the whole race of mankind, and let the world be filled with the knowledge of Thee and thy son Jesus Christ. Pity the sick, the poor, the weak, the needy, the widows and fatherless, and all that morn or are borken in heart, and be merciful to them according to their several necessities. bless my friends and grant me grace to forgive my enemies as heartily as I desire forgiveness of Thee my hevenly Father. I beseech thee to defend me this night from all evil, and do more for me than I ccan think or ask, for Jesus Christ sake, in whose most holy name & words, I continue to pray, Our Father, & c.

Tuesday Morning...

O Lord our God, most mighty and merciful father, I thine unworthy creature and servant, do once more approach thy presence. Though not worthy to appear before thee, because of my natural corruptions, and the many sins and transgressions which I have committed against thy divine majesty; yet I beseech thee, for the sake of him in whom thou art well pleased, the Lord Jesus Christ, to admit me to render thee deserved thanks and praises for thy manifold mercies extended toward me, for the quiet rest & repose of the past night, for food, rainment, health, peace, liberty, and the hopes of a better life through the merits of thy dear son's bitter passion. and O kind father continue thy mercy and favor to me this day, and ever hereafter; propse all my lawful undertakings; et me have all my directions from thy holy spirit; and success from thy bountiful hand. Let the bright beams of thy light so shine into my heart, and enlighten my mind in understanding thy blessed word, that I may be enabled to perform thy will in all things, and effectually resist all temptations of the world, the flesh and the devil. preserve and defend our rulers in church & state. bless the people of this land, be a father to the fatherless, a comforter to the comfortless, a deliverer to the captives, and a physician to the sick. let thy blessings guide this day and forever through J. C. in whose blessed form of prayer I conclude my weak petitions—Our Father, & c.

Tuesday Evening...

 Most gracious God and heavenly father, we cannot cease, but must cry unto thee for mercy, because my sins cry against me for justice. How shall I address myself unto thee, I must with the publican stand and admire at thy great goodness, tender mercy, and long suffering towards me, in that thou hast kept me the past day from being consumed and brought to nought. O Lord, what is man, or the son of man, that thou regardest him; the more days pass over my head, the more sins and iniquities I heap up against thee. If I should cast up the account of my good deeds done this day, how few and small would they be; but if I should reckon my miscarriages, surely they would be many and great. O, blessed father, let thy son's blood wash me from all impurities, and cleanse me from the stains of sin that are upon me. Give me grace to lay hold upon his merits; that they may be my reconciliation and atonement unto thee,—That I may know my sins are forgiven by his death & passion. embrace me in the arms of thy mercy; vouchsafe to receive me unto the bosom of thy love, shadow me with thy wings, that I may safely rest under thy suspicion this night; and so into thy hands I commend myself, both soul and body, in the name of thy son, J. C., beseeching Thee, when this life shall end, I may take my everlasating rest with thee in thy heavenly kingdom. bless all in authority over us, be merciful to all those afflicted with thy cross or calamity, bless all my friends, forgive my enemies and accept my thanksgiving this evening for all the mercies and favors afforded me; hear and graciously answer these my requests, and whaatever else thou see'st needful grant us, for the sake of Jesus Christ in whose blessed name and words I continue to pray, Our Father, & c.

A Prayer for Wednesday Morning...

Almighty and eternal Lord God, the great creator of heaven & earth, and the God and Father of our Lord Jesus Christ; look down from heaven, in pity and compassion upon me thy servant, who humbly prostrate myself before thee, sensible of thy mercy and my own misery; there is an infinite distance between thy glorious majesty and me, thy poor creature, the work of thy hand, between thy infinite power, and my weakness, thy wisdom, and my folly, thy eternal Being, and my mortal frame, but, O Lord, I have set myself at a greater distance from thee by my sin and wickedness, and humbly acknowledge the corruption of my nature and the many rebellions of my life. I have sinned against heaven and before thee, in thought, word & deed; I have contemned thy majesty and holy laws. I have likewise sinned by omitting what I ought to done, and committing what i ought not. I have rebelled against light, despised thy mercies and judgments, and broken my vows and promises; I have neglected teh means of Grace, and opportunities of becoming better; my iniquities are multiplies, and my sins are very great. I confess them, O Lord, with shame and sorrow, detestation and loathing, and desire to be vile in my own eyes, as I have rendered myself vile in thine. I humbly bessech thee to be merciful to me in the free pardon of my sins, for the sake of thy dear Son, my only saviour, I. C., who came not to call the righteous, but sinners to repentance; be pleased to renew my nature

and write thy laws upon my heart, and help me to live, right-eously, soberly, and godly in this evil worlds; make me humble, meek, patient and contented, and work in me the grace of thy holy spirit. prepare me for death and judgment, and let the thoughts thereof awaken me to a greater care and study to approve myself unto thee in well doing. bless our rulers in church & state. Help all in affliction or adversity——give them patience and a sanctified use of their affliction, and in thy good time deliverance from them; forgive my enemies, take me unto thy protection this day, keep me in perfect peace, which I ask in the name & for the sake of Jesus. Amen.

Wednesday Evening...

Holy and eternal Lord God who art the King of heaven, and the watchman of Israel, that never slumberest or sleepest, what shall we render unto thee for all thy benefits; because thou hast inclined thine ears unto me, therefore will I call on thee as long as I live, from the rising of the sun to the going down of the same let thy name be praised. among the infinite riches of thy mercy towards me, I desire to render thanks & praise for thy merciful preservation of me this day, as well as all the days of my life: and for the many other blessings & mercies spiritual & temporal which thou hast bestowed on me, contrary to my deserving. All these thy mercies call on me to be thankful and my infirmities & wants call for a continuance of thy tender mercies; cleanse my soul, O Lord, I beseech thee, from whatever is offensive to thee, and hurtful to me, and give me what is convenient for me. watch over me this night, and give me comfortable and sweet sleep to fit me for the service of the day following. Let my soul watch for the coming of the Lord Jesus; let my bed put me in mind of my grave, and my rising from there of my last resurrection; O heavenly Father, so frame this heart of mine, that I may ever delight to live according to thy will and command, in holiness and righteousness before thee all the days of my life. Let me remember, O Lord, the time will come when the trumpet shall sound, and the dead shall rise and stand before the judgment seat, and give an account of whatever

they have done in the body, and let me so prepare my soul, that I may do it with joy and not with grief. bless the rulers and people of this and forget not those who are under any affliction or oppression. Let thy favor be extended to all my relations friends and all others who I ought to remember in my prayer and hear me I beseech thee for the sake of my dear redeemer in whose most holy words, I farther pray, Our Father, &c.

Thursday Morning...

Most gracious Lord God, whose dwelling is in the highest heavens, and yet beholdest the lowly and humble upon the earth, I blush and am ashamed to lift up my eyes to thy dwelling place, because I have sinned against thee; look down, I beseech thee upon me thy unworthy servant who prostrate myself at the footstool of thy mercy, confessing my own guiltiness, and begging pardon for my sins; what couldst thou have done Lord more for me, or what could I have done more against thee? Thou didst send me thy Son to take nature upon

"The manuscript ended at this place, the close of a page. Whether the other pages were lost or the prayers were never completed, has not been determined."

George Washington's Adopted Daughter Discusses Washington's Religious Character

Woodlawn, 26 February, 1833.

Sir,

I received your favor of the 20th instant last evening, and hasten to give you the information, which you desire.

Truro Parish is the one in which Mount Vernon, Pohick Church, and Woodlawn are situated. Fairfax Parish is now Alexandria. Before the Federal District was ceded to Congress, Alexandria was in Fairfax County. General Washington had a pew in Pohick Church, and one in Christ Church at Alexandria. He was very instrumental in establishing Pohick Church, and I believe subscribed largely. His pew was near the pulpit. I have a perfect recollection of being there, before his election to the presidency, with him and my grandmother. It was a beautiful church, and had a large, respectable, and wealthy congregation, who were regular attendants.

He attended the church at Alexandria when the weather and roads permitted a ride of ten miles. In New York and Philadelphia he never omitted attendance at church in the morning, unless detained by indisposition. The afternoon was spent in his own room at home; the evening with his family, and without company. Sometimes an old and intimate friend called to see us for an hour or two; but visiting and visitors were prohibited for that day. No one in church attended to the services with more reverential respect. My grandmother, who was eminently pious, never deviated from her early habits. She always knelt. The General, as was then the custom, stood during the devotional parts of the service. On communion Sundays, he left the church with me, after the blessing, and returned home, and we sent the carriage back for my grandmother.

It was his custom to retire to his library at nine or ten o'clock where he remained an hour before he went to his chamber. He always rose before the sunand remained in his library until called to breakfast. I never witnessed his private devotions. I never inquired about them. I should have thought it the greatest heresy to doubt his firm belief in Christianity. His life, his writings, prove that he was a Christian. He was not one of those who act or pray, "that they may be seen of men." He communed with his God in secret.

My mother resided two years at Mount Vernon after her marriage with John Parke Custis, the only son of Mrs. Washington. I have heard her say that General Washington always received the sacrament with my grandmother before the revolution. When my aunt, Miss Custis died suddenly at Mount Vernon, before they could realize the event, he knelt by her and prayed most fervently, most affectingly, for her recovery. Of this I was assured by Judge Washington's mother and other witnesses.

He was a silent, thoughtful man. He spoke little generally; never of himself. I never heard him relate a single act of his life during the war. I have often seen him perfectly abstracted, his lips moving, but no sound was perceptible. I have sometimes made him laugh most heartily from sympathy with my joyous and extravagant spirits. I was, probably, one of the last persons on earth to whom he would have addressed serious conversation, particularly when he knew that I had the most perfect model of female excellence ever with me as my monitress, who acted the part of a tender and devoted parent, loving me as only a mother can love, and never extenuating or approving in me what she disapproved of others. She never omitted her private devotions, or her public duties; and she and her husband were so perfectly united and happy that he must have been a Christian. She had no doubts, no fears for him. After forty years of devoted affection and uninterrupted happiness, she resigned him without a murmur into the arms of his Savior and his God, with the assured hope of his eternal felicity. Is it necessary that any one should certify, "General Washington avowed himself to me a believer in Christianity?" As well may we question his patriotism, his heroic, disinterested devotion to his country. His mottos were, "Deeds, not Words"; and, "For God and my Country."

With sentiments of esteem,

I am,

Nelly Custis-Lewis

Coolidge Kneeling
in Prayer

S"ilent Cal" Coolidge is most often remembered for his reticence. *Coolidge: An American Enigma,* written by Robert Sobel, is the basis for an article written by Jeff Jacoby in the Boston Globe. Here is a fascinating excerpt from that article by Sobel:

"Seventy-five years ago, Calvin Coolidge was sworn in as the 30th president of the United States.....That night, back in 1923, was one of high drama. As President Harding lay dying in San Francisco, Vice President Coolidge was visiting his father and stepmother in the lonely Vermont village where he had grown up. There was no electricity in the house, no plumbing, no telephone. Light came from a kerosene lamp."

"Word of Harding's death reached White River Junction, the nearest large town, by telegram. By the time someone got the news to Plymouth Notch, it was extremely late. John Coolidge, the vice president's father, answered the knock at the door. In a trembling voice he called upstairs to his son."

"Coolidge and his wife returned to the bedroom," Sobel writes. "They washed, dressed, and knelt by the bed to pray. Then they went downstairs, where Coolidge dictated a message of sympathy to Mrs. Harding. The house was now crowded with reporters and others."

"The attorney general urged Coolidge to take the oath of office without delay. He "went across the street to the general store and telephoned Secretary of State (Charles Evans) Hughes, who informed him the oath could be administered by a notary. Coolidge returned home, and in the downstairs sitting room John Coolidge, using the family Bible, swore his son in as president. The time was 2:47 a.m."

Source: *75 Years of Underestimating Calvin Coolidge*, Jeff Jacoby, The Boston Globe, August 1998.

John F. Kennedy's Famous Line, "Ask not what your country..."

Kathryn Kay's poem "Thanksgiving Prayer" was probably the poem which inspired President John F. Kennedy's most memorial words: "Ask not what your country can do for you, ask what you can do for your country. "Thanksgiving Prayer" was published in Kay's book *If the Shoe Fits* in early November, 1941.

A few years after the death of President John F. Kennedy, Kathryn received a phone call from Charles Siems, a profession lobbyist in Congress in Washington, D.C. He called her to tell her of the connection of her "Thanksgiving Prayer" to President Kennedy's famous challenge. Charles reported that President Kennedy had stated that his famous couplet was inspired by a poem he had heard many years earlier on a Thanksgiving program, and that it had "stuck with him." Of course, he did not remember the name of the poem nor the author, but only the impact of the idea burning into his soul.

Charles pointed out to Kathryn that her poem almost certainly had to be the poem which inspired the president because it was heard across the country on Thanksgiving, and it emphasizes a very similar idea. Young John F. Kennedy had just graduated from Harvard at age 23

in June, 1940. At the time of the reading of "Thanksgiving Prayer" he was just at the impressionable age where he was beginning his career and was perhaps resolving to have America become as proud of him as he was of her. It is hard to estimate the impact on history that a single poem might have.

Thanksgiving Prayer

God, ev'ry year about this time,
according to routine,
I've bowed my head in the accepted way
and offered thanks, like some well synchronized machine
that prayed because it was the time to pray.
But, God, this year is different, this year I seem to feel
America's Thanksgiving is my own,
that in my nation's gratitude I have a part that's real,
a part that until now I've never known.
And, God, this year a deep humility has filled my heart,
a newborn pride rings true thruout my soul
because I do belong, because I have and am a part,
a tiny part of one tremendous whole.
I think I know the feeling of those first Americans
who said, "We must give thanks for this, our land."
I cherish now the rights that are each woman's, ev'ry man's,
the rights I've just begun to understand.
This year my heart has learned what all Thanksgiving Days are for,
true thankfulness at last I realize,
but, God, I'm sorry that it took the tragedy of war
in other lands to open up my eyes.
Again I bow my head but this time deep within me stirs
a mighty prayer, part of one vast design,
"God, help me make America as proud that I am hers—
as I am proud, and grateful she is mine!"

President's Gallery

George Washington

1st President of the United States
(1789–1797)

Religious background: Anglican

John Adams

2nd President of the United States
(1797–1801)

Religious background: Unitarian

Thomas Jefferson

3rd President of the United States
(1801–1809)

Religious background:
No formal affiliation

James Madison

4th President of the United States
(1809–1817)

Religious background: Episcopal

James Monroe

5th President of the United States
(1817–1825)

Religious background: Episcopal

John Quincy Adams

6th President of the United States
1825–1829)

Religious background: Unitarian

Andrew Jackson

7th President of the United States
(1829–1837)

Religious background: Presbyterian

Martin Van Buren

8th President of the United States
(1837–1841)

Religious background:
Dutch Reformed

William Henry Harrison

9th President of the United States
(1841–1841)

Religious background: Episcopal

John Tyler

10th President of the United States
(1841–1845)

Religious background: Episcopal

James K. Polk

11th President of the United States
(1845–1849)

Religious background: Presbyterian

Zachary Taylor

12th President of the United States
(1849–1850)

Religious background: Episcopal

Millard Fillmore

13th President of the United States
(1850–1853)

Religious background: Unitarian

Franklin Pierce

14th President of the United States
(1853–1857)

Religious background: Episcopal

James Buchanan

15th President of the United States
(1857–1861)

Religious background: Presbyterian

Abraham Lincoln

16th President of the United States
(1861–1865)

*Religious background:
No formal affiliation*

Andrew Johnson

17th President of the United States
(1865-1869)

*Religious background:
No formal affiliation*

Ulysses Grant

18th President of the United States
(1869–1877)

Religious background: Methodist

Rutherford Hayes

19th President of the United States
(1877–1881)

Religious background:
No formal affiliation

James Garfield

20th President of the United States
(1881–1881)

Religious background:
Disciples of Christ

Chester Arthur

21st President of the United States
(1881–1885)

Religious background: Episcopalian

Grover Cleveland

22nd, 24th President of the United States
(1885–1889, 1893–1897)

Religious background: Presbyterian

Benjamin Harrison

23rd President of the United States
(1889–1893)

Religious background: Presbyterian

William McKinley

25th President of the United States
(1897–1901)

Religious background: Methodist

Theodore Roosevelt

26th President of the United States
(1901–1909)

*Religious background:
Dutch Reformed*

William Taft

27th President of the United States
(1909–1913)

Religious background: Unitarian

Woodrow Wilson

28th President of the United States
(1913–1921)

Religious background: Presbyterian

Warren Harding

29th President of the United States
(1912–1923)

Religious background: Baptist

Calvin Coolidge

30th President of the United States
(1923–1929)

*Religious background:
Congregationalist*

Herbert Hoover

31st President of the United States
(1929–1933)

*Religious background:
Society of Friends (Quaker)*

From the Oval Office

Franklin D. Roosevelt

32nd President of the United States
(1933–1945)

Religious background: Episcopal

Harry Truman

33rd President of the United States
(1945–1953)

Religious background: Baptist

Dwight D. Eisenhower

34th President of the United States
(1953–1961)

Religious background: Presbyterian

John F. Kennedy

35th President of the United States
(1961–1963)

*Religious background:
Roman Catholic*

Lyndon Johnson

36th President of the United States
(1963–1969)

Religious background:
Disciples of Christ

Richard M. Nixon

37th President of the United States
(1969–1974)

Religious background:
Society of Friends (Quaker)

Gerald Ford

38th President of the United States
(1974–1977)

Religious background: Episcopal

Jimmy Carter

39th President of the United States
(1977–1981)

Religious background: Baptist

From the Oval Office

Ronald Reagan

40th President of the United States
(1981–1989)

Religious background:
Disciples of Christ

George Bush

41st President of the United States
(1989–1993)

Religious background: Episcopal

William J. Clinton

42nd President of the United States
(1993–2001)

Religious background: Baptist

George W. Bush

43rd President of the United States
(2001–?)

Religious background: Methodist